HAGGAI
and
MALACHI

by

HERBERT WOLF

MOODY PRESS
CHICAGO

© 1976 by
THE MOODY BIBLE INSTITUTE
OF CHICAGO

5 6 7 Printing/EP/Year 87 86 85

Library of Congress Cataloging in Publication Data

Wolf, Herbert, 1938-
    Haggai and Malachi/by Herbert Wolf.—Chicago: Moody Press, c1976.
    128 p.; 19 cm.—(Everyman's Bible commentary)

    Bibliography: p. 128.
    ISBN 0-8024-2037-0

    1. Bible. O.T. Haggai—Commentaries. 2. Bible. O.T. Malachi—Commentaries. I. Title. II. Series.
BS1655.3W58   224'.97'07   76-35692

Contents

Preface

HAGGAI AND MALACHI are two postexilic minor prophets who address key issues faced by both the Church and the home today. Attitudes, priorities, the use of money, and the problem of divorce are some of the practical areas brought into sharp focus. Important passages on the second coming of Christ are also included.

Though authored some eighty-five years apart, these concise books show remarkably similar theme and style. While Haggai successfully attempts to challenge the Jews returned from exile to rebuild the Temple, Malachi chides them for their severe moral and spiritual breakdown, which includes the pollution of that same sanctuary so recently constructed to aid their corporate worship. In Haggai the people rally in response to the prophet's message, but in Malachi they argue with God. The priests play an important role in both books. True to prophetic practice, Haggai and Malachi also contain passages looking forward to the last days and to the rule of the Messiah.

A stylistic feature common to each book is the skillful use of rhetorical questions posed by God to His people. Through penetrating interrogation, God probes the hearts of His reluctant followers and provides compelling answers. While more frequent and well known in Malachi, this questioning technique has telling force in Haggai also.

According to some interpreters, these two prophetic gems belong to a list of seven Old Testament books with no poetic lines. The parallelism which characterizes Hebrew poetry may in some cases be identified in Malachi, but "elevated prose" probably best describes the style of both Haggai and Malachi. The messages are unadorned but hard-hitting.

Jewish tradition asserts that Haggai and Malachi, along with Zechariah, were instrumental in the founding of the "Great Synagogue," an assembly of godly scholars credited with preserving the Old Testament books.

HAGGAI

1

Introduction to Haggai

Historical Background

WHEN THE BABYLONIAN ARMY completed its divinely appointed
task of destroying Jerusalem with its sacred Temple in 586 BC,
the Jewish people faced years in captivity that threatened to wipe
out their nation and religion. Without the Temple, so central to
their whole way of life, the Jews had no rallying point to bind
them together. It was the Temple toward which they had prayed,
and, indeed, Solomon had instructed them to direct their prayers
to Jerusalem and the Temple even if they found themselves held
captive in a foreign land (1 Kings 8:48; Jon 2:7). Thus it was
with heartfelt joy that the Jews heard the decree of Cyrus, King
of Persia, allowing the return to Palestine to rebuild the Temple
in 538 BC. This Persian conqueror of Babylon, by reversing the
deportation policies of the Assyrian and Babylonian empires,
paved the way for Zerubbabel to lead some 50,000 Jews back to
Palestine.

Upon their arrival in Jerusalem, all efforts were directed toward the construction of the sacred shrine. Using Phoenician
materials and workmen, even as Solomon had done, the people
were able to lay the foundation of the Temple about two years
after their return (Ezra 3:8-10). This important milestone led
to rejoicing and praising God, because the Jews were well aware
what a restored Temple would mean for the entire Dispersion.

Unfortunately, the Samaritans who had resided in Palestine

since the seventh century also sensed something of the political significance of that Temple. After an unsuccessful attempt to join ranks with the Jews, the rejected Samaritans used terrorist tactics to bring to a halt the building so auspiciously started. Their opposition included direct appeals to Cyrus and his successor, Cambyses, to warn of the "rebellious tendencies" of the Jews. Persian pressure was evidently brought to bear upon the returnees, which, coupled with Samaritan harassment, dashed the hopes of the Jews for a quick Temple completion. From 536 to 520 the work stalled, and the Jews seemed resigned to this sad state of affairs.

When Darius the Great assumed the throne in 521, the Jews themselves were more to blame for their inactivity than their angry opponents. Darius showed interest in religion throughout his empire, and the Jews should have sensed that the opportunity to resume their labors was at hand. Instead, they were strangely satisfied to exist without a center for worship. Spiritual paralysis had set in, and it was to arouse them from this lethargy that Haggai emerged with his powerful preaching.

The prophet. Apart from the book that bears his name, Haggai is mentioned only in Ezra 5:1 and 6:14. There, he is linked with Zechariah, son of Iddo, his much younger contemporary, who aided him in the task of proclaiming God's message concerning the Temple. In Ezra 5:2 the prophets are credited with valuable support in the building project. Zechariah and Haggai are again joined together in the Septuagint, which attributes Psalms 145-148 to these prophets. Other versions also relate Haggai to the writing of a few psalms. The tradition may reflect the keen interest of the prophetic pair in the worship of the second Temple.

The name *Haggai* means "festal" and is derived from the word *hag,* "feast, festival," which usually refers to the three pilgrimage feasts of the Jewish religious calendar. It may be that Haggai was born during one of these festal celebrations (Feast of Unleavened Bread, of Weeks, of Tabernacles). Since the name of his father is not given, Haggai may have come from a family of humble origins.

Based on Haggai 2:3, several commentators have inferred that the prophet was one of those who had seen the splendor of Solomon's Temple prior to 587. If this is true, Haggai must have been about eighty years old when he prophesied, a factor that may account for his very brief ministry.

Date and style. This compact prophecy ranks next to Obadiah as the shortest book in the Old Testament. It was the first prophetic work of the postexilic period, and there is happily no quarrel between liberals and conservatives as to the date of writing. Haggai himself assigns a date to each of his four messages, ranging from the first day of the sixth month (August-September) to the twenty-fourth of the ninth month (November-December), all coming within the second year of Darius Hystaspes (520 BC). Thus, the entire book covers only a four-month span.

Not infrequently the style of Haggai has been disparaged for its lack of brilliance and poetic flair. Judging from the effectiveness of this brief book, however, one dare not criticize him too harshly. The concise message preached vigorously in the power of God was more successful than many a longer prophetic work.

The prophet spoke authoritatively, claiming five times that he was declaring the word of the Lord. In 1:1, 3, and in 2:1, the Lord's word came literally "by the hand of" or "through" Haggai, while the expression used in 2:10 and 20 states that the word came "to" Haggai. Further emphasis on the source of his message is found in 1:13, where the prophet speaks "by the commission of the LORD." His was a divine imperative.

Repetition of words and phrases is carefully interwoven into the book. Several times (1:1, 12, 14; 2:2, 4) Zerubbabel, the governor, and Joshua, the high priest, are linked with the people or the remnant of the people in the same verse or context. Yet in 2:21-23 Zerubbabel alone is addressed, and the contrast may be significant. Twice in Haggai the expression "Consider your

ways" (lit., "Set your heart upon your ways") occurs (1:5, 7).
An additional two times the same "Set your heart" appears in
the clause "Consider from this day onward" (2:15, 18). Early
in the book, the prophet also uses repetition to bemoan the fact
that the Lord's house lay desolate (1:4, 9). Then, in 2:6 and 21,
we find the identical line, "I am going to shake the heavens and
the earth."

As mentioned in the preface, rhetorical questions are sprinkled
throughout the book. Usually it is the Lord who asks the question
either of the people in general (1:4, 9; 2:3, 19) or of the priests
(2:12-13). The first two questions sound the harshest notes, as
Haggai probes the souls of this people so slow to complete their
divinely appointed task.

Another stylistic feature relates to allusions or quotations from
other canonical books. Haggai effectively draws upon several
verses found in Deuteronomy 28. Compare Haggai 1:6 with
Deuteronomy 28:38-40 and especially 2:17 with Deuteronomy
28:22. In the latter pair, "blasting wind" and "mildew" are
identical in each passage. The prophet is clearly reminding the
people of the curses threatened by Moses, which had indeed
brought distress to the returned exiles. In 2:4 the thrice repeated
imperative, "Take courage," reflects the same word found in
Joshua 1:9. Directed toward another Joshua, the son of Jehozadak and the high priest, this exhortation is most appropriate.

Outline of Haggai

I. First Message: The Challenge to Build the Temple (1:1-11)
    A. Introduction (v. 1)
    B. God Answers the People's Excuse (vv. 2-4)
    C. God Sums Up the Plight of the People (vv. 5-6)
    D. God Gives Reasons for Their Distress (vv. 7-11)

2

First Message

I. FIRST MESSAGE: The Challenge to Build the Temple (1:1-11)

THE OPENING VERSES of Haggai present a frontal attack by the prophet against the nation that had failed to rebuild the Temple. The people's excuses are exposed, and their present miseries, both material and spiritual, are traced directly to a lack of obedience in this single area.

A. Introduction (v. 1)

Haggai immediately introduces the reader to the main characters of the book via this precisely dated formula. The first message, like the other three, is delivered during the second year of Darius Hystaspes (521—486 BC), king of the Persian empire, and usually called "the Great."

Darius took the throne after killing his brother Smerdis who was really an impersonator, according to Darius. Sensing a weakness in Persian power, many smaller nations launched rebellions, which Darius systematically subdued down to 519. His victories are recorded on the Behistun rock, a trilingual inscription which led to the deciphering of the ancient cuneiform languages of Mesopotamia. The small territory of Judah did not participate in these revolts, and it is to the credit of Darius that, in the midst of his battle to consolidate the empire in 520, he permitted the Jews to rebuild the Temple.

The fact that Haggai began his ministry in the sixth month reflects careful timing. This was the month called "Elul," corresponding to our August and September. It followed the month of Ab, the very time that Nebuchadnezzar captured Jerusalem and leveled Solomon's Temple. To this day, Jews gather at the Wailing Wall by the thousands on the ninth of Ab, standing before those stones built by Herod to support the Temple area, to mourn the fall of the Temple. Strangely enough, the Temple that Haggai pleaded for and which Herod the Great beautified, fell to the Romans in the same month of Ab, AD 70. Perhaps the mourning for bygone Temple glories spurred Haggai to present his challenge at this time. Two months later, Zechariah began his prophetic ministry (Zec 1:1).

The first day of the month also lent itself to spiritual concerns. This was the "New Moon" holy day, when business activities were suspended as on the Sabbath (Amos 8:5) and a special burnt offering was brought to the Lord (Num 28:11-15). Apparently it was also an occasion to listen to the prophets (2 Ki 4:23).

Lest the people think they were sampling some prophet's uninspired opinion, Haggai identifies the message as the word of the Lord. The entire book is punctuated with "thus says the LORD" (1:2, 7, 13; 2:4, 6-9, 11, 14, 23), for the prophet is merely the instrument through whom the Lord speaks. At times in the Old Testament, the prophet is so closely identified with God that it is difficult to decide which one is speaking. God has given the prophet a message, so the prophet speaks as if he were God.

The recipients of the message are the civil and ecclesiastical leaders of Judah, Zerubbabel and Joshua. Five times these two names appear together, and each time Zerubbabel is mentioned first (see also Zec 4:11-14). By directing his statements to the leaders, Haggai underscores their responsibility. Perhaps the leaders, as well as the people, had lost the vision of the completed Temple and needed a rebuke from God. Elsewhere (in 2:2 and 4) the people are addressed along with the two heads, but in 1:1 only the leaders are approached.

Zerubbabel, son of Shealtiel, had been the leading figure in the return from exile ever since the decree of Cyrus in 538 (Ezra

2:1-2). As a descendant of David, his royal lineage was a key
factor in his leadership and in the Messianic associations of his
name in Haggai 2:20-23.

He appears in the genealogies of Matthew 1 and Luke 3, and,
together with the records in 1 Chronicles 3:17-19, several problems are faced. In Chronicles, Zerubbabel is the son of Pedaiah
(brother of Shealtiel) and grandson of King Jeconiah (also
called Jehoiachin). In Luke 3 he is said to be the son of Shealtiel
(as in Haggai six times) but the grandson of Neri. These com-
plications are probably due to the practice of levirate marriage
and the differences between legal and actual sons. Zerubbabel
was probably the natural born son of Pedaiah and the legal son
of Shealtiel. Similarly, Neri was most likely his natural grandfather, but childless King Jeconiah enters the picture by adop-
tion. Either way, Zerubbabel is descended from David, whether
through Solomon or Nathan, and this is the important point.[1]

Zerubbabel is also to be identified with Sheshbazzar of Ezra
1:8, 11, and 5:14, 16. Sheshbazzar is called "the prince of
Judah" (Ezra 1:8) and "governor" (Ezra 5:14), using the same
word applied here to Zerubbabel. Just as Daniel was called
Belteshazzar in Babylon, so Zerubbabel, meaning in Hebrew
"seed of Babylon," or, "born in Babylon," also was given the
name Sheshbazzar. When Cyrus or other Persian officials are
mentioned in the context, "Sheshbazzar" is the name employed.[2]

Although Zerubbabel is called "governor of Judah," he is sub-
servient to the governor of the province "beyond the River,"
who in turn may have been responsible to the satraps of the Persian empire (Ezra 5:3). This particular term for governor
(*pehah*) was a carry-over from Assyrian and Babylonian rule.
By the days of Nehemiah, a Persian word for governor was employed (Neh 8:9).

Joshua, the son of Jehozadak, is mentioned right after Zerubbabel, just as he is in the list of those returning from the exile in

1. See Richard Wolff, *The Book of Haggai*, pp. 23-25, for further possibilities.
2. Theodore Laetsch, *The Minor Prophets*, p. 383.

Ezra 2:2. His father had been taken into captivity by Nebuchadnezzar (1 Ch 6:15), and his grandfather, Seraiah, met death at
the hands of that same monarch at Riblah (2 Ki 25:18-21).
Seraiah had been called the "head priest" (first-ranking priest),
whereas Joshua bears the title of "great priest," a form also used
consistently in Zechariah (3:1, 8). The two titles are synonymous, but "great priest," often translated "high priest," pre-
dominates in the postexilic books. Joshua, called "Jeshua" in
Ezra and Nehemiah, was the first high priest after the exile.

B. God Answers the People's Excuse (1:2-4)

Haggai's first words to the people lay bare the lame excuse that
stymied the building operation: the right time to rebuild the
Temple had not come. It was not Haggai who was quoting the
people, however, but God, the LORD of hosts, who was well
aware of men's puny rationalization. "LORD of hosts" is used
several times in Haggai, building to a climax in a twofold usage
in the last verse. A title never used in the Pentateuch, it appears
more than eighty times in the postexilic prophets, Haggai, Zechariah, and Malachi. Properly it means "LORD of armies," as seen
in Isaiah 13:4 where "the LORD of hosts [armies] is mustering the
army." The "army," or "host," can refer to the angels, the stars,
or the nation Israel. God controls all of them, and yet here the
all-powerful One confronts a reluctant nation.

The Lord refers to the nation as "this people" rather than "My
people." They do not deserve to be called His because of their
persistent sin. Jeremiah also uses "this people" as a term of
reproach (Jer 14:10, 11).

Essentially the excuse amounted to procrastination. When a
more convenient time came, they would consider resuming the
task, but not now. Perhaps they were waiting for improved
economic conditions (1:6, 11) or for the cessation of opposition
from unfriendly neighbors. Besides, things were unsettled in
Persia with the stormy accession of Darius. Some may even have
based their argument on scriptural grounds, for Jeremiah had

prophesied a seventy-year captivity, and only sixty-seven years
had elapsed since Jerusalem fell. Whatever their reasons, the
people were neglecting the one task to which they had been commissioned by God and Cyrus.

The Temple is frequently called the Lord's "house" in Haggai.
Eight times this designation appears (1:2, 4, 9, 14; 2:7, 9),
while twice the word *hekal,* meaning "temple" or "palace," is
employed (2:15, 18).[3] In a real sense God had made Solomon's
Temple His dwelling place on earth. He "lived" there and had
filled the building with His glorious presence.

With stinging force, the word of the Lord came through Haggai
to refute the people in 1:4. If it is not time to build the Lord's
house, how have you managed to construct your own paneled
houses? The selfishness of the people is stressed by the repeated
pronoun "for you yourselves." Unlike David, who, in 2 Samuel
7:2, lived in a cedar house but longed to build a Temple for God,
these people think only of themselves. And at least the Lord had
a tent in David's day. Now the Temple was desolate, a waste,
just as Jerusalem was ruined by conquest (Neh 2:3, 17). The
word *desolate* is closely related to the Arabic word "Khirbet" of
"Khirbet Qumran," the abandoned ruins about seven miles south
of Jericho where the community which preserved the Dead Sea
Scrolls once lived.

Not only were the people able to build houses, but they were
paneled ones at that. Paneling connoted luxury and is in fact
usually associated with royal dwellings, such as the palace built
by Solomon (1 Ki 7:3, 7; cf. Jer 22:14). These homes were
paneled with cedar, and, although the specific wood is not mentioned in Haggai, it might have been the famed cedar of Lebanon
that is intended. We are told that Zerubbabel and Joshua did
purchase cedars from Lebanon for the Temple upon their return
from exile (Ezra 3:7). Could it be that the construction delay
on the Temple had tempted the Jews to use the valuable cedar

3. *Hekal* actually is derived from an ancient Sumerian word that literally
means "big house."

on their own homes rather than letting it go to waste? Perhaps the possibility of giving up on the Temple project is too cruel a deduction, but Malachi does ask the sad question, "Will a man rob God?" (Mal 3:8).

Since the kind of wood used for the paneling is not specified, one might interpret "paneling" as "ceiling," because the literal meaning of the word is only "covering." This sense appears in 1 Kings 6:15, a passage describing the construction of Solomon's Temple. God's complaint could then be that the people had a roof over their heads, while He had none. Some sixteen years previously, the foundation of the Temple had been laid, but there the work stalled. None of the people's houses had been left in such an incomplete state. Having a ceiling would not connote the luxury implied by cedar paneling, and in view of the poverty owing to drought and famine described in verses 6-11, such an interpretation might be preferable.

The failure to put God first in one's life is unfortunately not confined to the distant past. Several years ago, I attended a summer conference of Russian Evangelicals, many of whom had spent long, difficult years in European displaced persons camps. The speaker that week referred to the promises made by many Christians under those trying circumstances. They told God that if He would allow them to come to America, their lives would be devoted to Him in faithful service. Yet the minister was bemoaning the fact that several of those same refugees owned three houses in America and were negotiating for a fourth, but they had not begun to serve God with any consistency. How easy it is to forget one's spiritual vows and be caught up in materialism and personal pursuits. Like the immigrants, many of us born in America are more concerned with developing our own interests than with building the church of God.

C. God Sums Up the Plight of the People (1:5-6)

In view of the selfish choice made by the people, God reviews for them their deplorable economic condition. This is introduced by the imperative "Consider your ways!" in verse 5. Literally, "Set your heart upon your ways," the words are asking for a re-appraisal of their situation. They are to take a close look at things, just as God asked Satan to consider His servant Job (Job 1:8), where the same idiom occurs, though with opposite intent. Hebrew frequently uses *heart* where we would use *mind*. Although *heart* can refer to the seat of emotions, it is usually closely related to the intellectual aspect of man. Thus, Deuteronomy 6:5 can speak of loving the Lord "with all your heart," while verse 6 refers to words that should be on one's heart. The second instance we would more naturally translate as "mind." The Lord, through Haggai, is pleading with the people to see the results of their attitudes and actions and then to reconsider their behavior.

With succinct descriptions, Haggai summarizes the frustrations of the community in verse 6. In spite of generous planting of seed, the harvest is meager. This is a theme reiterated in 1:10-11 and 2:15-17, verses which imply that crops had been poor for years. It is an economic disaster which the prophet summarizes by using the emotionally charged construction. There is not enough to eat or drink or wear. Although food, drink, and warm clothes have to do with the necessities of life, the expression used with regard to drinking is especially poignant. The text states that the amount they had to drink was not even enough to get drunk on, perhaps to drown out their present woes. This does not mean that Haggai approved of drunkenness any more than Hosea condoned immorality in Hosea 4:10. In that passage, the eighth-century prophet lists as punishment for Israel, "They will eat, but not have enough; They will play the harlot, but not increase." Like Haggai, Hosea links the legitimate with the illegitimate to show futility in all areas of life.

Under such conditions, those who earned wages labored largely in vain also. It was like putting money into a purse with holes in it, for prices rise sharply in time of famine. Leviticus 26:20 speaks of expending energy for nothing because of the unfruitfulness of a land plagued by God.

The plight of the people is very similar to what Moses predicted as a curse for disobedience in Deuteronomy 28:38-40. Those verses also describe a small harvest and the failure of vineyards and olive trees. Deuteronomy 28:41, moreover, foresees the captivity of the Israelites' sons and daughters as further punishment. How amazing that those so recently returned from exile in Haggai find themselves subject to the same curses of people threatened with captivity centuries earlier! It was as if God were preparing to send them back into exile, so serious were their sins.

D. God Gives Reasons for Their Distress (1:7-11)

Now that the Lord has outlined the sad results of their sin in verse 6, the people may be more inclined to respond to the second occurrence of "Consider your ways." To help bring about the desired change, God makes explicit the command only implicit in verses 2-4: "Go up to the mountains, bring wood and rebuild the temple" (v. 8). Since the word *mountains* is actually singular, some have suggested that Mt. Moriah or the Lebanon range is in view. Ezra 3:7 does record the purchase of cedar wood from Lebanon when they had first returned to Jerusalem, and it is possible that more was required. It is possible that no trees large enough for construction timbers for the Temple grew in Palestine. In any event, the splendid cedars of Lebanon would have been preferred.

Tuland suggests that the wood of verse 8 was to be found in Palestine, but that it would be used for scaffolding and not for lumber.[4] Others support the view that "the mountain" refers to the hills around Jerusalem, since the same collective use of the singular occurs in Nehemiah 8:15. If the cedars ordered in Ezra 3 were still on hand, perhaps any additional wood needed could have been found in the surrounding area. God's command implies that timber was available if they would begin to work in earnest on the divine project.

4. C. G. Tuland, *Journal of Near Eastern Studies,* 17 (1958), p. 274.

Building the Temple in obedience to the Lord would be pleasing to Him. He would take delight in His completed house, just as He accepts suitable sacrifices, and the word for "to be pleasing" is, in fact, often used of receiving sacrifices. Malachi complains that the offerings of the people are emphatically unacceptable (1:8, 10, 13). Perhaps God is referring to the Temple as the product of a living sacrifice, acceptable to Him (Ro 12:1-2). It required dedicated work but was clearly the good and perfect will of God for them.

Construction of the Temple would bring glory to God also. By obeying His command, the Jews would declare to the world that their God was worthy of a dwelling place where He could be worshiped. To glorify God is to honor Him, and the Hebrew word used can be translated either "glorify" or "honor." Parents deserve the honor and respect of their children (Ex 20:12), and God, as the heavenly Father, commands even greater honor. In actuality, the rebuilding of the Temple would signify the reestablishment of the nation, thereby strengthening it. The Jewish nation and their God would gain respect in the eyes of the world. Isaiah 26:15 similarly links the extension of the borders of Israel with the glorification of God. In a sense, God's glory depends on the status of Israel. When that nation clings to Him in obedience, God receives praise and glory (Jer 13:11). If they are rebellious and God is compelled to punish them, His own reputation is tarnished.

A restored Temple with its renewed sacrificial system was another practical means of glorifying God—provided that an obedient people offered proper sacrifices. First Corinthians 6:19-20 also speaks of the possibility of glorifying God in His temple, namely in our bodies, the temple of the Holy Spirit.

Almost anticipating possible objections to the challenge of verse 8, the Lord abruptly returns to the present sad situation of the people in Judah. Their expectations for bountiful crops are high, but the results are small. And even the little that they are able to bring home evaporates before the Lord. God "blows into it," and everything disappears. The idea behind the metaphor of "blowing" is most likely "to blow away" forcefully, even as God blows upon Israel to melt them in the fire of His wrath (Eze 22:21). Another interpretation treats "blow" as "to sniff at disdainfully," based on the usage in Malachi 1:13. A different form of the verb is employed there, however.

Why does God deplete their resources? It is because His house lies in ruins, while their individual homes are cared for. This is an emphatic restatement of verse 4, except that it places God's house in the first clause rather than the second. The people "are running" to their own houses, a description expressing enthusiasm and speed in handling any home-improvement projects. Proverbs 1:16 and Isaiah 59:7 speak of feet that run to evil. Men are quick to get in trouble or to serve their own interests, but they move slowly and laboriously in the work of God. Time and money are carefully rationed when it comes to serving the Lord.

Faced with such attitudes and actions, God took certain steps, which explains the distress of verses 6 and 9a. Why are the harvests so meager? God has withheld His "showers of blessing" to render the land unfruitful. Verse 10 mentions specifically that the sky has withheld its dew. Dew was normally plentiful and almost as important as rain. When there was no dew or rain, this was viewed as a terrible curse (1 Ki 17:1). After the death of Saul and Jonathan, David prayed that the mountains of Gilboa would have no rain or dew, in effect cursing that area (2 Sa 1:21). Deuteronomy 28:23-24 forcefully describes the curse of drought, when the sky becomes bronze and the earth iron, so that the only rain is powder and dust. Under those conditions the rock hard soil is "restrained" from producing anything. Ironically, the verb *withhold,* or *restrain,* which appears twice in this verse, is used in Genesis 8:2 of the rain of heaven being restrained to end the flood. There it marked the end of a curse; here it marks the beginning, as the windows of heaven are locked tight. And the reason why God has suspended His blessing is

also given: "because of you" and your sinful ways, seen in verses
4 and 9. Do not blame God; it is your own fault.

The word for "drought" in verse 11 means "dryness" and then
"desolation, ruins." It is closely related to the word used to
describe the desolate Temple in verses 4 and 9 (see comments
on 1:4). If they choose to leave the Temple essentially in ruins,
they deserve to be ruined also. God "called for a drought" just
as He "called for a famine upon the land" in the days of Joseph
(Ps 105:16; cf. 2 Ki 8:1). The verb expresses the power of the
word of God, who is able to call the world into existence or to
call men into His service (Is 48:15). He had called to the people
of Judah, but they had not responded; so now He summons
nature, which cannot resist Him.

The drought is due to hit the entire land, including the soil and
crops, the animals who pasture there, and the men who live from
its produce. Mountains are mentioned because so much of Judah
is hilly and because this was valuable land for cultivation. In
several passages, Scripture speaks of the fruitful terraced vineyards in the mountains (Is 7:25; Joel 3:18).

The produce of the land is specified as grain, wine, and oil.
These were the three basic crops of Palestine, and they are frequently mentioned together in the same order. Particularly in
Deuteronomy is this trio of staples linked together in passages
relating to the blessing or cursing of Israel. When the nation
obeyed God, rain would fall to increase their grain, wine, and oil
(Deu 11:14), but during times of rebellion, a foreign power
would consume these crops (Deu 28:51; cf. Deu 7:13; 12:17;
14:23). The grain refers most likely to barley or wheat, while
the oil denotes olive oil used for food, ointment, or medicine.
Although the word for wine (*tirosh*) is not as common as the
word used in 2:12, it occurs consistently in this threefold combination. It is often translated "new wine," but it can be as intoxi-
cating and harmful as any other wine (Ho 4:11).

Since *drought* can be translated as "dryness" or "fever" (Job
30:30), the "drought upon men and cattle" includes sickness and

disease (Deu 28:22) as well as other afflictions. It very likely refers to an inability to reproduce also, because Deuteronomy 7:13-14 speaks of blessing upon their grain, wine, and oil and of the multiplication of both man and beast—blessing on the fruit of the womb along with the fruit of the ground. Conversely, a curse reducing the number of crops would also reduce the number of offspring. Barrenness was the rule. Whatever man attempted to produce, in fact, would be barren, for the drought would fall "on all the labor of your hands." "Labor" can refer to the toil or to the result of the toil, the product. Exertion was useless, because in the end everything would wither away.

By so clearly drawing the attention of the people to the curses of Deuteronomy, the prophet is underscoring the magnitude of their sin. Such a plight suited a nation about to go into exile, not one barely back in the homeland.

Verses 7-11 also vividly illustrate the relationship between the spiritual and the material. Those who put self before God are not really gaining wealth and comfort. They are losing things along with their spiritual vitality. On the other hand, when believers wholeheartedly give resources and energy to the Lord's work, often God blesses in a material way also. The principles of giving seen in Malachi 3:8-11 are paralleled by Haggai.

II. POSITIVE RESPONSE OF ZERUBBABEL AND THE PEOPLE (1:12-15)

Haggai's strong words in verses 1-11 demanded a decisive response. Either the people would resist the Lord even more stubbornly and rid themselves of the troublesome prophet, or they would acknowledge their sin and commit themselves to build the long-awaited Temple. It was a crucial decision.

A. The Leaders and People Listen and Obey (1:12)

Rarely in prophetic annals has such a short message received such a favorable and dramatic response. Though brief, Haggai's message was powerful, and the whole community took up the

challenge. Zerubbabel and Joshua, the leaders to whom the
prophet spoke directly in verse 1, are fittingly the first to respond.
Normally, where these two men are referred to in the same verse,
Zerubbabel's office as governor of Judah is also mentioned (1:1,
14; 2:2), but here, in verse 12, and in 2:4, the title is omitted.
Perhaps Zerubbabel is not responding as governor but as an individual who needs to repent. Joshua, however, is called "the
son of Jehozadak, the high priest," and this full title is used consistently whenever Joshua is mentioned in Haggai.

The leaders were not alone in their reaction to the prophet,
for right along with them are "all the remnant of the people." The
entire group was unified in its desire to do God's will. "Remnant"
refers to what is left over after a tragedy or a time of testing.
"Rest" or "remainder" are other possible renderings. In regard
to Isaiah, the remnant can refer to the people left in the land after
military invasion (Is 37:4; Jer 40:11) or to those survivors
scattered on foreign soil (Jer 8:3). Often, *remnant* is something
of a technical term for the faithful few within the nation (Mic
5:7, 8), but it can refer to a wicked segment of the populace also
(Jer 8:3).

In Haggai the "remnant" means those who had returned from
exile and who should have been conspicuous as the faithful of
God. Only from this point on, however, were they behaving like
the godly corps implied by the term *remnant*.

The people and their leaders listened to the voice of the Lord,
which is the normal Hebrew idiom for obeying the Lord. One
has not really listened to what God has to say until obedience
takes place. Conversely, one can hardly obey until there is opportunity to hear the word of God. In this case, the voice of God
is clearly equated with the words of Haggai. Since God had sent
His prophet and had spoken through him, the prophet's words
were the very words of God. The people accepted the authority
of Haggai's message on that basis.[5]

5. For a practical application, see *Four Minor Prophets* by Frank Gaebelein,
   p. 217.

By their positive response, the people "feared the LORD," or, "showed reverence for the LORD." Instead of shrinking from their task for fear of hostile neighbors, the returned exiles began to fear the One whose power was far greater. They had a new awe, a new reverence for the God who shakes heaven and earth and overthrows kingdoms and nations (2:6, 22).

It is impossible to fear God properly without obeying Him, and in verse 12, the two ideas are inseparable. Abraham proved that he feared God by being willing to offer Isaac on the altar of sacrifice, thus obeying the voice of God (Gen 22:12, 18). For Abraham, this meant loving God more than himself or his own family. To fear the Lord is to love Him and obey Him with wholehearted devotion.

B. The Lord Empowers the Workers (1:13-15)

Prior to verse 13, the words spoken by Haggai had been harsh and judgmental, so it must have been with a sense of deep gratitude and joy that he is commissioned to present a different kind of message to a changed and responsive audience. The only time in the book Haggai is called "the messenger of the Lord" is in verse 13. Some have questioned the authenticity of this title, but it can be used to refer to prophets (2 Ch 36:15) and priests (Mal 2:7). In Malachi 3:1, "My messenger" is a reference to the coming of John the Baptist, and the meaning of the name "Malachi" is "My messenger." The same word can also mean "angel," and the term "the angel of the LORD" usually refers to the preincarnate Son of God (Gen 16:9, 13; 22:15; Ex 3:2). Though Haggai is certainly not being called an angel, the fact that the identical words can mean "the angel of the LORD" indicates the high and holy calling of a human prophet. He too is sent by God to minister to the people.

Since the men of Judah had been rather indifferent to the work of the Lord for over fifteen years, they may have been somewhat apprehensive about the Lord's response. Would He accept them and assist them in their new resolve, or would further reproof fall from the lips of Haggai? God's reply is short, yet significant: "I am with you." This is the basic meaning of the personal name of God, "Yahweh," which is known more commonly as "Jehovah." The Lord would be on their side to help them against all foes.

In Numbers 14:9, Joshua and Caleb challenged the Israelites not to delay their invasion of Canaan for fear of the people of the land. They were no match for Israel because "the LORD is with us."

Isaiah confronted Ahaz with the sign of Immanuel, "God is with us," in an unsuccessful attempt to keep that ungodly king from trembling before his enemies (Is 7:3-14).[6] If God is for us, who can be against us? (Ro 8:31)

Jacob received a similar promise that the Lord would be with him when he was told to leave Laban and go back to Canaan, though this meant facing Esau (Gen 31:3).

So there is little doubt that these few words from the Lord, repeated in 2:4, brought great encouragement to the people.

Evidence of the Lord's presence is seen in verse 14 as He "stirred up the spirit" of Zerubbabel, Joshua, and of all the remnant. The threefold occurrence of *spirit* emphasizes this work of God on the inner man. The same idiom of "stirring up" or "arousing the spirit" occurs in Ezra 1:5, where the Lord was motivating the leaders of families and the priests and Levites to leave their exilic homes and to rebuild the Temple in Jerusalem. It was largely the same individuals who felt God's urging in 538 BC who sensed anew the exciting tug of His Spirit in 520, and the object of that "stirring up" remained the same.

Deuteronomy 32:11 compares God to an eagle stirring up its nest and fluttering over its young. As the eagle gets its eaglets moving, so the Lord carries and leads His people. He awakens them out of their lethargy to accomplish His purposes. Several times, Scripture speaks of God "stirring up the spirit" of heathen

6. See my article, "A Solution to the Immanuel Prophecy in Isaiah 7-8," in *Journal of Biblical Literature* (December 1972): 449-56.

kings to carry out His will by invasion. God aroused the spirit of the Medes to overthrow the Babylonian empire (Jer 51:11). Great emotion and energy is involved in such undertakings, but the results are outstanding.

Empowered by God, the people began actual work on the Lord's house; the project was underway once again. It may be significant that the word *work* comes from the same root as the words *messenger* and *commission* in verse 13. Haggai had done his work of proclaiming God's word well. Perhaps it was more difficult for him to preach than to labor physically, but his work paved the way for theirs.

Not until the people are obedient to the Lord do they call Him "their God." In verse 12, where they turned back to God, and again in verse 14, the same phrase occurs for the third time. They had no right to assume He was "their God" until they began to listen to Him and straighten out their relationship with Him.

Twenty-three days after the Lord's message had been given to them by Haggai, the work on the Temple began. This three-week delay may not indicate a slow response to the challenge but rather a time for planning and organization. Materials had to be gathered or at least dusted off, and some expert craftsmen needed to be hired (cf. Ezra 3:7).

The date formula of verse 15 is the only one in Haggai which is not attached to "the word of the Lord came to Haggai" (see 1:1; 2:1, 10, 20). This factor, and the occurrence of consecutive date verses (1:15 and 2:1) has led some scholars to suspect textual corruption. Their suggested improvements are unconvincing, however, and the text seems reasonable enough as it stands. It is true that the date usually comes at the start of a sentence, but 2:20, like 1:15, varies the order.

3

Second Message

III. SECOND MESSAGE: The Glory of the New Temple Defined (2:1-9)

FIRMLY COMMITTED to build the Temple, the people were soon to face some difficult questions. How beautiful would this Temple be? How would its glory compare with Solomon's Temple? In chapter 2 the Lord encourages them with a promise of unexcelled glory for the new structure.

A. Comparison with Solomon's Temple (2:1-3)

Haggai delivered only one message to stir the people to action, but three messages were necessary to encourage them. The first of these is dated significantly on the twenty-first day of the seventh month, less than a month after work on the Temple had resumed. Tishri, as the seventh month was commonly called, fell within our September-October and was an important religious season. The climax of the religious observances came during the Feast of Tabernacles, or Booths, one of the three annual pilgrimage festivals, which lasted from the fifteenth to the twenty-first of the month. It commemorated the wilderness wanderings after release from Egypt and also celebrated the ingathering of the summer harvest (Lev 23:34-43). Since a drought had ruined the crops for the returned exiles, this may have been a most discouraging time for them. They also knew that Solomon had dedicated his Temple at this feast in the seventh month (1 Ki 8:2), and it was already clear that their Temple would suffer in comparison with Solomon's majestic one.

The twenty-first day ended this religious festival and was a particularly fitting time for Haggai to address the people. In John 7:37, Jesus selected "the last day, the great day of the feast" of Tabernacles to offer living water to those in spiritual drought. To those experiencing a literal drought, Haggai directs his words of encouragement on this strategic religious holiday.

The closest parallel to this event on the American scene is Thanksgiving, where a recently gathered harvest is also associated with religious and national celebration. The returned exiles were not exactly pilgrims coming to a new continent, but they were attempting to get reestablished in familiar territory. It was a season to bring back memories of joy and plenty, though under difficult circumstances it readily led to deep discouragement. Imagine celebrating Thanksgiving without turkey or dressing!

The date formula of 2:1 follows closely the arrangement in the opening verse of the book, and the recipients of the message are the same also. Since the intent of the Lord's words is encouragement, not condemnation as in chapter 1, an introductory "Speak now," or "Please speak," softens the address in verse 2. In chapter 1, the message was directed only to Zerubbabel and Joshua, and the people were sharply differentiated as "this people." But here "the remnant of the people," having responded in obedience, are included along with their leaders.

Through a series of questions in verse 3, Haggai brings to the surface a key problem felt by the people. As work progressed and plans were formed for the new Temple, inevitable comparisons were made with Solomon's glorious structure. That first Temple had been destroyed sixty-six years previously, and some of the older men, perhaps including Haggai himself, could vividly remember its beauty. How could they possibly produce such a fine building now? It was the same reaction recorded in Ezra 3:10-13, when the foundation of the Temple was laid the second year after the return from exile. There was great rejoicing, but those who had seen Solomon's Temple wept profusely. By this time even fewer of these men were alive, but the same mixed feelings prevailed.

Haggai shows the continuity between the Temples by describing Solomon's structure as "this temple in its former [or first] glory." Although the time from the construction of Zerubbabel's Temple until the destruction of AD 70 is known in history as the period of the second Temple, in a very real sense, it was an extension of the first Temple. There is a unity to the Temple throughout history, whatever the outward form. The timeless use of "this house" appears again in verses 7 and 9.

"Glory" is associated with "splendor," "riches," and "honor" (see notes on 1:8). Sometimes it can specifically mean "wealth," as in Genesis 31:1, and it is often linked with material riches (1 Ch 29:12). The house of the Lord is the place where His glory is manifest (Ps 26:8), frequently identified with the cloud which filled the Temple (1 Ki 8:10-11). Thus, "glory" can refer to material splendor as well as to the presence of God, though at this stage in the reconstruction process, the people saw little of either aspect. Comparison with the previous splendor of the Temple was inherently dangerous, because the elderly could dishearten and annoy the young with descriptions of "the good old days." Ecclesiastes 7:10 warns against this common fault.

The fact that this Temple had barely been started may account partially for Haggai's strong assertion that there was no comparison whatever between this building and Solomon's. Materials may have been in short supply, for no "wealthy and honorable" king had made extensive preparations as David did for his son Solomon in 1 Chronicles 22, 28, and 29. Instead, resources seemed very limited.

B. Encouragement for the Builders (2:4-5)

Along with the problems already enumerated, Ezra informs us that opposition to the Temple rebuilding arose from Tattenai, governor of the province "beyond the River," and from other officials (Ezra 5:1—6:13). Just as the people of the land had successfully stopped the work some sixteen years earlier, so now important individuals blocked the project. A letter was written to King Darius, who studied the decree of Cyrus and authorized the completion of the Temple.

Haggai says nothing about this opposition, so it may have been only a potential danger in the early months of the work. Yet Zerubbabel and the others doubtless expected such organized attempts, and the encouragement of Haggai prepared them to meet the challenge head on.

Three times in verse 4 the prophet repeats the words, "Take courage" (or, "Be strong"), once to Zerubbabel, then to Joshua, and to all the people of the land. This is followed by the plural imperative addressed to all three: "and work." By repeating "Take courage," Haggai may be recalling the threefold command given not to Joshua, son of Jehozadak, the priest, but to Joshua, son of Nun, the successor of Moses (Jos 1:6-9), who was faced with many overwhelming problems.

More specifically, Haggai is probably reflecting upon David's charge to Solomon to build the Temple. In 1 Chronicles 28:10, 20 David uses both words found in 2:4 to challenge his wise son: "Take courage and act" (or, "work"); carry out the Temple project because my God is with you (v. 20). The same words, "I am with you," so important in Haggai 1:13, occur also in 2:4. Just as David told Solomon to act with determination in completing the first Temple, so the Lord uses the very same language to stir the people to carry out the work of rebuilding. The task may be harder now, but the same God will supply the power. The combination "take courage and act" is also used in Ezra 10:4, where Shecaniah asks Ezra to take decisive action to bring a later generation of returned exiles back into fellowship with God.

The tasks God assigns to His people today may not be of the magnitude of Solomon's Temple. Yet it is just as important for us to complete our assignments as it was for either Solomon or Zerubbabel to finish his building project. The scope of the responsibility may differ, but the same mighty Lord is with us to provide all the strength we need.

Unlike the first three instances where Zerubbabel, Joshua, and "all the remnant of the people" are linked in the same verse (1:12, 14; 2:2), Haggai uses "all the people of the land" for the populace in general. Perhaps the change implies that the Lord considers them firmly in possession of their land, while "remnant" could convey a weak and scattered status. Whatever the reason, "remnant" does not occur again in Haggai.

It is clear that verse 5 continues the encouragement of verse 4, but the relationship between the two is difficult. The concluding "Do not fear" is connected with the idea of "Take courage," for in the passages where "Be strong and courageous" occurs, the statement, "Do not be afraid or dismayed" is in the immediate context (Jos 1:9; 1 Ch 28:20). The way to overcome fear is to take heart in the Lord.

A reference to the past provides additional strength for the people, as Haggai recalls promises God made when He freed Israel from Egypt. Covenant relationship is in view, for verse 5 literally speaks of "the word I cut with you," and the expression "to cut a covenant" is the normal Hebrew idiom for making a covenant. Here "word" is substituted for "covenant" to emphasize the verbal communication. Animals were sometimes cut in two during the covenant ceremony as a sign that a similar fate would befall anyone violating the terms of the covenant (see Gen 15:8-18). The promise so firmly attested is either "I am with you" of verse 4 or the similar "My Spirit is abiding in your midst" of verse 5. Just as the Holy Spirit was with them when God brought the nation through the Red Sea (Is 63:11), so that same Spirit would empower them under Zerubbabel and Joshua.

Emphasis upon the work of the Spirit also stands out in the book of Haggai's contemporary, Zechariah, where that prophet records the famous words, "Not by might nor by power, but by My Spirit" (4:6). In Haggai, the Spirit is said to be "abiding," or "standing," in their midst. The same word in Exodus 8:22

(v. 18 in Heb. text) is equivalent to "living." God the Spirit is very much alive among them. He will stand His ground and lead them in their important work, so why be afraid?

C. God's Supply of Glory for the New Temple (2:6-9)

With these verses we come to the heart of the message and to probably the most difficult portion of the book. The verses tell us why the Temple is eminently worth rebuilding and how its glory relates to Solomon's magnificent structure. Messianic elements and distant predictions are involved in the interpretation as well.

The section begins with, "Thus says the LORD of hosts." Verse 4 had recorded "declares the Lord" three times, and now verses 6-9 repeat the same idea five times. This marks the greatest concentration of references to divine authority in Haggai.

The background to verse 6 is similar to that of verses 4 and 5, namely, the Exodus from Egypt and the covenant promises related to Mt. Sinai. At Sinai the voice of the Lord caused an earthquake, and a thunderstorm shook loose the rains (Ex 19:16-20). Psalm 68:8 (v. 9 in Heb. text) refers to the earth quaking and the heavens dropping rain in that wilderness experience. Hebrews 12:26, quoting Haggai 2:6, also compares this shaking of heaven and earth with that great theophany at Sinai. The reference to the sea and dry land implies some connection to the crossing of the Red Sea, one and a half months before Israel arrived at Sinai. Just as God brought judgment on Egypt by sending Israel across the Red Sea, so He will once again reveal Himself in awesome power as He judges all the nations.

The relationship between the judging of nations and the shaking of heaven and earth is established by Haggai 2:7 and 21-22, which explicitly speak of shaking the nations and overthrowing kingdoms. Isaiah 14:16-17 also describes the king of Babylon as one who "shook kingdoms" and "overthrew . . . cities," and in Ezekiel 31:16, the nations "quake" at the downfall of Egypt. Clearly, the collapse of political structures as a result of the judgment of God has something to do with the interpretation.

When, however, will all this upheaval take place? Finding the
answer is not easy, particularly because in quoting Haggai, the
writer of Hebrews followed the Septuagint, and the Greek omits
"in a little while" from its text. Thus, Hebrews 12:26-27 emphasizes the expression, "Yet once more," with its eschatological
import. There is little doubt that the ultimate fulfillment of the
passage awaits the second coming of Christ, when indeed the
kingdoms of this world will become the kingdom of our God.
Joel 3:16 (4:16, Heb. text) connects the shaking of heaven and
earth with the roaring of God against the nations that are attack-
ing Jerusalem. Similarly, Isaiah 13:13 ties the trembling of the
world to the day of the Lord (Is 13:9), using description similar
to the book of Revelation. It will be an awesome, cataclysmic
shaking.

A passage vital to the understanding of these verses in Haggai
is Isaiah 60:1-9. There, the prophet is also talking about the
shaking of nations and the bringing of glory to God's house.
Isaiah 60:5b is particularly pertinent: "Because the abundance
of the sea will be turned to you, The wealth of the nations will
come to you." The verb *will be turned* is the same one found in
Haggai 2:22, where the statement, "I will overthrow the thrones
of kingdoms" is directly linked with "I am going to shake the
heavens and the earth" (v. 21). In Isaiah 60:5 the "turning" or
"overthrow" refers partially to the enrichment of Israel by the
nations during the kingdom period. This enrichment is very
likely in view in Haggai 2:6-7 also. The "sea" is parallel to
"nations" in Isaiah 60:5, and the same correspondence occurs
in Haggai 2:6-7. Thus, after the cataclysmic shaking accompa-
nying the Lord's judgment, the wealth of the nations will be
"turned over" to Israel.

Yet one can scarcely relegate all of this "shakeup" to the distant future, because Haggai 2:6 includes the expression "it is a
little," meaning, "in a little while." Parables, such as Jeremiah
51:33, almost demand such a temporal rendering, one which
implies a "near fulfillment" within the foreseeable future. Jere-

miah predicted that Babylon would be judged after the "little while" of some fifty years, and it may be that Haggai has reference to the fall of the Persian empire and the rule of the Greeks and Romans. God is the One who "removes kings and establishes kings" throughout history (Dan 2:21).

In the light of Isaiah 60:1-9, the near fulfillment may include reference to the financial help given to the Temple project by King Darius. Ezra 6:8-9 records the decree of the Persian king reinforcing the initial decree of Cyrus (Ezra 6:3-5) to that effect. This "turnover" of resources to the Jews foreshadows the future contributions of Isaiah 60:5.

The precise significance of "shaking all the nations" would be understood if the interpretation of verse 7 were clearer. Unfortunately, great difference of opinion has prevailed about this crucial verse because of grammatical difficulties and what may be the intentional ambiguity of the author.

The translation of the first clause is clear enough, although, as it has been pointed out, the meaning of "shake all the nations" has two aspects. Here the agreement ends, and the translation of the next few words is a battleground. The King James rendering, "The desire of all nations shall come," has been challenged by later translations. The American Standard Version (1901) changed "desire" to "precious things," while the New American Standard Bible now reads, "They will come with the wealth of all nations." The New English Bible has, "The treasure of all nations shall come hither," and the New American Bible uses "treasures." Obviously the trend has been away from the possible Messianic "desire" toward the impersonal concept of valuable things.

The reason for the controversy is the use of a plural verb, *come,* with a singular noun, *desire,* which may have the collective idea of "desired things." Having pointed this out, most commentators immediately eliminate any reference to a person.[7] The

---

7. One who still retains the personal element is Charles Feinberg in the *Wycliffe Bible Commentary,* p. 893.

problem is far more complicated, however, because by substitut-
ing different vowels, the noun can also be plural and can agree
with the verb in number. It is a well-known fact that the vowels
are a later addition to the text of the entire Old Testament, and in
Haggai 2:7, the early Greek translation (the Septuagint) took
this word as a plural. If both the noun and the verb are plural,
the construction can refer to a person, just as the statement "God
revealed Himself" in Genesis 35:7 has a plural noun and verb.
But since the word *God,* "Elohim," is plural in form,[8] the verb
can also be plural, while at the same time referring to only
one person.

Actually, both the singular and the plural form of *desire* are
used in Scripture with reference to persons. First Samuel 9:20
speaks about "the desire of Israel" being directed toward Saul,
and Daniel 11:37 mentions "the desire of women," probably
referring to a god in which women delight. The plural of the
same word (*hamudoth*), having the very same consonants as in
Haggai 2:7, is used three times to describe Daniel himself. In
Daniel 9:23 he is called "highly esteemed," or, more literally,
"desirability" or "preciousness." Twice in chapter 10 (vv. 11
and 19) Daniel is called "man of high esteem," literally, "man of
preciousness." Another possible use of this plural noun to describe a person occurs in Genesis 27:15, where Esau, rather than
his garments, is the "desirable one," the "highly esteemed one" in
Isaac's opinion.

It is equally true that both the singular and plural forms of this
noun are used with reference to valuable possessions, especially
silver and gold. Frequently the idiom "vessels of desire" is employed. This idiom, with the singular, occurs in 2 Chronicles
32:27 ("valuable articles") and 36:10, and in Daniel 11:8
("precious vessels"). The same idiom with the plural noun is
found in 2 Chronicles 20:25 ("valuable things") and in Daniel
11:43 ("precious things"). To sum up, whether singular or

8. Grammarians call this a "plural of majesty," or an "intensive plural" which
views the various characteristics of Deity as a unity.

plural, the noun means something like "preciousness," and it can refer to either highly valued persons or possessions. Probably both ideas are intended in 2:7.

Parallel passages provide strong evidence that the concept of valuable treasures is included here. In the previously cited Isaiah 60:5, one finds, "The wealth of the nations will come to you." As in Haggai 2:7, "wealth" is singular and "will come" is plural, presenting a grammatical difficulty. Like the word *desire* or *preciousness,* "wealth" in Isaiah 60:5 (*hayil*) can also have a personal reference, for it can mean "array, force." Yet the context shows that "wealth" is the primary meaning, and Zechariah 14:14 describes "the wealth of all the surrounding nations" in terms of silver and gold and garments.

Why does Haggai not use the same term for wealth as Isaiah and Zechariah, since silver and gold are in the context here (2:8) also? Most likely he selected *preciousness* because it afforded the exact ambiguity he desired, while the other term for "wealth" (*hayil*) would exclude the personal reference.

Ultimately it does apply to the gathering of the treasures of nations after the second coming of Christ and to "the glory and honor of the nations" in the new Jerusalem (Rev 21:26), but it can also refer to that "treasure" or "desire of nations" who is "the messenger of the covenant in whom you delight" (Mal 3:1).

Ever since Abraham's day, the world has awaited the One in whom "all the families of the earth shall be blessed" (Gen 12:3). Though the nations may not have recognized Him when He became incarnate, yet He is the only One who can fulfill their desire for peace on earth (2:9).

Another example of a double meaning in verse 7 is the term *glory.* The word can refer equally well to material splendor or to the presence of God (see notes on 1:8 and 2:3). Verse 8 tips the scales in favor of material glory, but verse 9 favors the personal aspect.

When Christ entered the Temple in the first century, the Lord's house was filled with glory as it had never been before. Strictly

speaking, wherever God fills His house with glory in the Old
Testament, a visible cloud signifying the presence of God enters
the sanctuary (Ex 40:34-35; 1 Ki 8:10-11). Verse 7 does not
say that God will fill His house with "the glory of the Lord." But
the only glory said to "fill the temple" in Scripture is the Shekinah
glory itself. Isaiah 60:7 connects the wealth of the nations with
the glorifying of His house (see Is 60:13 also), but can material
splendor alone fill the Temple with glory? There is more than a
hint that the personal presence of God is also necessary.

When the child Jesus was brought to the Temple by Mary and
Joseph, the aged Simeon expressed his profound thanks to God
for permitting him to see His salvation. He identified Jesus with

> "A LIGHT OF REVELATION TO THE GENTILES,
> And the glory of Thy people Israel" (Lk 2:32).

Perhaps the "glory" associated with Christ's presence in the
Temple was in the mind of the prophet Haggai also.

The "shaking of the nations" would result in the beautification
of the Temple. But in verse 8, the people are reminded that God
does not depend on anyone else to supply resources. From the
divine perspective, all silver and gold belongs to Him. Money
is no problem to God, so the Jews should not doubt His ability
to provide the necessary materials.

After amassing vast amounts of silver and gold and other
precious goods, David acknowledged that "all things come from
Thee." God had given David and Solomon the resources to build
the first Temple through military victory and trade, and the same
Lord could use different means to supply the materials for the
rebuilding of His house.

If the first stage in the fulfillment of verses 6-9 relates to
Zerubbabel's Temple, there is another sense in which the silver
and gold belongs to God. Cyrus had ordered that the very gold
and silver articles taken from the Temple by Nebuchadnezzar be
returned to Jerusalem (Ezra 6:5), and Darius commissioned his
officials to pay the cost of rebuilding the Temple out of the royal

treasury (Ezra 6:8). These steps involved reparations to the Jewish people for the Babylonian destruction of the Temple. The Persians were returning the resources that rightfully belonged to the Jews and their God.

In verse 9, Haggai brings to a climax this section of encouragement (vv. 4-9) by explicitly stating that the latter glory of this house would be greater than the former. Another possible translation for these words is, "the glory of this latter house," which would make the two "houses" the point of the contrast. Verse 3 decides the issue in favor of the first interpretation, since it refers to "this temple in its former glory." The relative "glories" are being contrasted, not two Temples; for the Temple in its various forms is viewed as one throughout the course of history (see comments on 2:3 also). Yet, the alternate translation would not change the meaning, since it is the glory of Solomon's Temple which fails to measure up to the glory of Zerubbabel's Temple.

Some commentators feel that Haggai is alluding to the present meager glory of Zerubbabel's Temple as opposed to the later beautification of this Temple by Herod.[9] But the statement takes on greater significance if *Solomon's* magnificent structure were somehow to be outshone, especially in light of the dismal prospects of verse 3.

The interpretation of verse 7 has already given my explanation of such a startling promise. Part of the fulfillment came with the first coming of Christ, who as God incarnate and One "greater than Solomon" (Mt 12:42), brought glory into the Temple whenever He visited there. More complete fulfillment awaits the second coming of our Saviour, when the nations will bring their wealth to Jerusalem to glorify His sanctuary, a later form of "this house," at the inauguration of the Kingdom of God (Is 60:7, 13).

The second coming of Christ ties in best with the last part of the promise: "In this place I shall give peace" (v. 9). "This place" is not the Temple alone, but Jerusalem, the holy city. Again, parallel passages illuminate the meaning, for after verses

9. See Jack P. Lewis, *The Minor Prophets*, p. 72; and Laetsch, p. 397.

describing the shaking of the nations and the glorification of the Temple, these chapters go on to speak about peace in Jerusalem. Violence and destruction will be over (Is 60:18), and never again will foreigners invade her land (Joel 3:17, 20 [Heb. text: 4:17, 20]). Spiritual peace is of course included, but "peace on earth" will actually be realized in its fullest sense. On this exultant note, the second message comes to a close.

4

Third Message

IV. THIRD MESSAGE: The Building of the Temple Reverses Israel's Fortunes (2:10-19)

IN SPITE of the stirring promises of Haggai 2:1-9, the small nation was still living with the consequences of their prolonged sin. Harvests had been pitifully small, so that food remained scarce. But from now on, God assures them, all this will be changed. His blessing will rest upon them, and future crops will be plentiful.

A. The Contagious Nature of Sin (2:10-13)

Haggai's third message closely follows the structure of the message in 1:1-11. The formula, giving the date when the word of the Lord came to Haggai, introduces each section. This is followed by a censure of the past behavior of the people (1:2-4; 2:11-14), leading to the key phrase, "Consider your ways" (1:5; 2:15). In chapter one, their economic plight is attributed to their failure to build God's house, while in 2:15-19, those same agricultural woes fade before the promise of God's blessing.

The date assigned to this third message, the twenty-fourth of the ninth month, is exactly three months after the people had begun the rebuilding project in response to Haggai's initial challenge. It also follows by a little more than two months the strong encouragement given at the Feast of Tabernacles. The ninth month overlaps our months of November and December and came approximately during the planting season. Grain and other winter crops were sown then, since the fall rains usually ended the summer drought toward late October.[10]

Haggai implies that these abundant rains had come, but patience would be needed before the harvest (cf. v. 19). Perhaps some had concluded that the "little while" of 2:6 had elapsed without the expected results.

Unlike the headings in 1:1 and 2:1, where the "word of the LORD came by [or through] Haggai," in 2:10 the word comes "to" the prophet. The same preposition is used in the final heading (2:20), and it may indicate a more restricted audience than the previous addresses. This is easier to prove in 2:20-21, where Zerubbabel is the sole recipient of the message, though the priests as a single group are emphasized in 2:10-19.

Thus far in his short book, Haggai has asked several rhetorical questions; but now the Lord directs him to elicit (from the priests) a specific response to a legal question. The priests had been the legal experts in the land since Moses' day, commissioned to teach the Law to the nation. Whenever anyone had a question pertaining to the Mosaic Law, a priest was the one to consult (Deu 33:8-10; Mal 2:7). Prophets received new revelation from God, while the priests had the final word about the meaning of the Law (Jer 18:18). So Haggai is not after a "ruling" as much as a precise understanding of a particular aspect of the Law.

The occasion reminds one of our Lord's visit to the Temple in Luke 2:46, where He listened to the words of the teachers and asked them questions. Perhaps similar problems were being discussed then.

The question posed by Haggai concerns the transmission of holiness (v. 12) and of uncleanness (v. 13), both of which received considerable attention in the Pentateuch. Is it possible for holy meat, that is, meat set apart for a sacrifice, to communicate its holiness to other food while wrapped in the fold of a garment? The priests reply in the negative, showing that they knew what the Law says on this point. Leviticus 6:27 teaches that if anyone

10. See the *Interpreters Dictionary of the Bible,* 1:58-60.

touches holy meat *directly* he will become holy, but nowhere does Scripture say that *indirect* contact will sanctify a man. If a man touches something that has been in contact with holy meat, he does not thereby "catch" that holiness. The garment in which the meat was wrapped became holy, but it could not pass it on to a third object.[11]

Several words for "food" are used in this verse, because Haggai will soon refer to the "unholy" crops that have been so meager. The word for "cooked food" or "boiled food" is the type of thing one eats during a famine (2 Ki 4:38-39), and the people may have tasted that "stew" far too often during their lean years of disobedience.

When it came to uncleanness, however, the transmission process was more pervasive, particularly if one touched a dead body. Though the text literally speaks of someone "defiled of soul," passages like Numbers 9:10 employ the same idiom, obviously referring to a "dead soul," that is, a corpse. Coming in contact with a dead body brought severe defilement and could be removed only by special purifying water after a seven-day period (Num 19:11-13). Meanwhile, anything that an unclean person touched became unclean, ceremonially defiled (Num 19:22). This explains the Jewish tendency to avoid dead bodies, and the priests were under orders not to approach the dead unless close relatives were involved (Lev 21:1-4).

It is clear, then, that the ritual pollution contracted from touching the dead could be transmitted to a third party, whereas the sacred meat could not do this. The power of defilement is far easier to communicate than holiness. One can catch a cold from someone else, but it is impossible to catch the health of another. In the moral and spiritual sphere, Scripture teaches that the sin of Adam has contaminated the entire human race, but believing parents cannot transmit their saved condition directly to their children. Like physical diseases, sin is all too contagious, and it is best to avoid every form of evil (1 Th 5:22).

11. See Eze 44:19 and 46:20 on the transmission of holiness.

So the priests were again correct when they answered Haggai's second question with one Hebrew word: "It will become unclean." Since biblical Hebrew has no word for "yes," the priests' repetition of Haggai's statement is equivalent to a simple yes in English.

B. The Unclean Condition of Israel (2:14)

Haggai now applies the principles of the last two verses to the nation itself, for they also are carrying something holy in the fold of a garment while at the same time they are tainted with sin.

The precise correlation between the examples of verses 12-13 and the nation, as well as the time period intended, are difficult to determine. Most commentators feel that the "holy meat" corresponds to the "holy place," the sanctuary which the prophet has urged them to rebuild. One of the Hebrew words for the Temple is *miqdash*, "holy place, sanctuary," a term closely related to the "meat of holiness" of verse 12. The Temple, being sacred, could transmit its holiness to the land of Palestine, but it could not make the *products* from that land holy any more than the garment brushing against bread, wine, or oil could sanctify that food. The land had a measure of holiness since the foundation of the Temple years earlier, but this did not prevent a blight upon the crops of the land.

Apparently, the uncleanness referred to, which affected everything they did, was derived from a failure to complete the Temple. Unnecessary delays reflected sinful disobedience, so that even the sacrifices offered there, on the rebuilt altar, were regarded by the Lord as polluted.

Like the other prophets, Haggai gives potent emphasis to the fact that performance of rituals is not in itself a guarantee of divine favor. Acceptance depends upon the condition of the heart and the obedience of the people to all the will of God. (See also Is 1:11-17; Mal 1:7-8.)

Is Haggai saying, however, that in spite of the resumption of the Temple rebuilding, the people are still plagued by sin and disregarding the Lord? Most translations handle verse 14 in the present tense, but it could also be understood as, "So it was with the people," rather than, "So it is." Verse 15, with its opening, "But now," seems to contrast the past of verse 14 with the more hopeful present and future of verses 15-19. Haggai could hardly be asserting that sin has prolonged the famine, because too few months had intervened for the new crops to grow. As in verse 17, the prophet is glancing back at spiritual conditions that prevailed before the repentance recorded in chapter one.

Another factor linking verse 14 with their prior disobedient state is the expression "this people," which was used in 1:2 with a decidedly derogatory flavor. "This people" and "this nation" imply a time when Israel did not deserve the title, "My people." Some suggest that "this nation" refers to the Samaritans, who, as an unclean people, will pollute the sanctified Jews, whereas the Jews cannot purify them. Yet such an interpretation does not seem to agree with the total meaning of verses 12-14, and there is no evidence that the Samaritans offered to help in the days of Haggai.

C. Economic Disaster for Failure to Build Temple (2:15-17)

Using language reminiscent of 1:9-11, Haggai reviews for the people the judgment of the Lord upon the produce of the land. This historical flashback is introduced with the words, "Do set your heart," or, "Do consider." Here in verse 15 and again in verse 18, this expression is softened by the particle of entreaty, translated "please" or "do." Back in 1:5 and 7 the command "consider" was harshly given, with no little *do* added to blunt its force. There its intent was to condemn; here, it is designed to encourage.

The phrase, "From this day onward," poses a problem, because these three verses look into the past. Some change "onward" to "backward" in order to gain the historical perspective. The word is literally "upward," which could be ambiguous, but in usage, as in 1 Samuel 16:13 and even Haggai 2:18, the future "onward" or "forward" is clearly intended. Since verse 18 does repeat the entire phrase, the intervening material starting with "before one stone" may be parenthetical, and it is this material which emphasizes the past.

The sad conditions the prophet is about to relate deal with the period before stone was laid upon stone in the Temple. This refers to the time preceding the resumption of the work a few months earlier. Zerubbabel had laid the foundation, but there had been no building upon that foundation. Perhaps the mention of "one stone . . . upon another" emphasizes that the task would be slow, though every stone contributed to the whole. Peter speaks about believers as "living stones" who are being built as a spiritual house (1 Pe 2:5).

Likewise, Paul uses the imagery of a temple to warn the Corinthians about building wood, hay, and straw upon the foundation, which is Christ. Such materials will vanish in the flame, while gold, silver, and *precious stones* will endure (1 Co 3:10-14). Prior to the preaching of Haggai, the returned exiles had built nothing of value upon the Temple foundation.

As noted in the introduction, verses 15 and 18 employ a different word for "temple." Up to this point, *house* has been the standard designation, but now a word which can also mean "palace" is used. Haggai may be stressing God's position as King of the universe, One whose house should indeed be a palace. Another factor, more evident in verse 18, is the reference to the laying of the foundation years earlier. Ezra 3:10 records the completion of that notable phase in the project and uses the same word for "temple" (*hekal*) found in Haggai 2:15 and 18.

Before rebuilding efforts had been resumed, the people were constantly disappointed about their harvests. The results never matched the expectations. When they judged that a certain heap of sheaves would produce twenty measures of grain, they discovered after the winnowing process that it yielded only ten measures, a fifty percent loss. "Measures" is not actually in the text but is probably correctly supplied, based on such passages as 1 Samuel 25:18. One measure (Heb., *seah*) equaled about a half bushel.

Grape production was even worse, dropping to forty percent, as only twenty of the anticipated fifty measures materialized at the wine vat. The wine vat was a trough or reservoir often carved out of rock (Is 5:2), into which the juice flowed from the higher winepress where the grapes were trampled. The word for "measure" can also mean "winepress" or "trough" (Is 63:3), perhaps equaling the amount of juice "generally obtained from one filling of the winepress with grapes."[12]

The percentages achieved were certainly not encouraging, but they far exceeded the conditions described in Isaiah 5:10, where the amount of grain and wine to be received was only a tiny fraction of what might be expected normally. Verse 16 further explains just how "little" were the harvests bemoaned back in 1:6.

Such pitiful crops were caused by the relentless striking of the Lord's hand against the land. Just as Haggai had linked his first message to the curses predicted in Deuteronomy 28 (see 1:6, 10, 11), so again he turns to the very same passage. Deuteronomy 28:22 contains two of the three terms used in Haggai 2:17, the "blight" or "blasting wind" and the mildew. These two words occur together in the same verse and the same order three other times in Scripture: 1 Kings 8:37; its parallel, 2 Chronicles 6: 28; and Amos 4:9. The New American Standard Bible is consistent in its rendering of "mildew" (*yeraqon*), but uses "blasting wind," "scorching wind," and "blight" for *shiddaphon*. The "blight" was caused by the blasting of the east wind coming from the hot desert. Called the *khamsin* in Arabic today, this scorching wind blasted the ears of grain in Pharaoh's dream (Gen 41:6).

12. Carl Friedrich Keil, *The Twelve Minor Prophets,* pp. 206-7.

The word for "mildew" is less familiar, though again directed at crops. It can mean "pale green" and is applied once to faces turning pale, in Jeremiah 30:6. Perhaps its meaning should be linked more directly to the blasting wind.

Hail is not mentioned in Deuteronomy, but it does occur as an instrument of God's judgment in several Old Testament passages (Ex 9:25; Is 28:2; 30:30). God sent hail as one of the plagues against Egypt, and significantly, 1 Kings 8:37 and Amos 4:9-10 mention the word *plague* right after speaking of "blight and mildew." Hail is especially appropriate in 2:17, because God used it to destroy the vineyards in Egypt (Ps 78:47-48), and Haggai has just referred to the shortage of wine in 2:16. These particular plagues are hardest on grain and grapes.

Actually, "every work of your hands" is said to be smitten by God. In verse 14 the prophet expelled "every work of their hands" as unclean. It was their sin that blighted whatever they touched and brought on the judging storms of God. When one looks at the terrible crop failures caused by drought and at the floods hitting various nations today, one wonders how much of this is punishment for sin.

For years, God's judgment did not turn the people back to Him. They hardened their hearts, like Pharaoh and the Egyptians. At this point Haggai again has in mind Amos 4:9, which mentions the blight and mildew and the similar response of an earlier generation: "Yet you have not returned to Me." How often the prophets talk about the Lord's desire to lead His people to repentance. All that He says and does is directed to that end, but wayward Israel—like modern man—usually turned to their idols and their favorite sins instead of to God (Jer 3:6-10; 4:1).

D. Economic Blessing Accompanies Temple Building (2:18-19)

Fortunately, the curse of poverty under the judging hand of

God was a thing of the past, as the prophet resumes the opening line of verse 15: "Do consider from this day onward." Life will be different because we are once again obeying the Lord. To underscore the difference between the past and future, Haggai stresses the exact date that this message from the Lord was received, namely, the twenty-fourth day of the ninth month (see v. 10).

Then the prophet mentions a second day, and this reference has stymied many interpreters. Why does Haggai talk about the day when the foundation of the Temple was laid? A rapid reading of the text leads one to conclude that the twenty-fourth of the ninth month was indeed the day the foundation was laid.[13] Yet Ezra 3:10-12 describes the laying of the Temple foundation back in 536 BC. Had that foundation been destroyed during the intervening years, or was this a second dedication of the same foundation?

Happily, Hebrew grammar rescues us from the dilemma because the word *from,* connected with the laying of the foundation, always refers to a point in the past leading up to the present. In other words, one could translate, "Since the day when the Temple of the Lord was founded (until now), consider." Passages such as Judges 19:30 or Jeremiah 7:25 and 32:31 illustrate this usage. The verse in Judges is particularly helpful: "Nothing like this has ever happened . . . from the day when the sons of Israel came up from the land of Egypt to this day. Consider it." Like Haggai, the writer of Judges includes an expression for "consider" after outlining the time interval. In Judges, the people of Israel are bemoaning the horrible rape-murder perpetrated by the tribe of Benjamin. Nothing that bad had happened before. Haggai also notes that nothing good has charac-

13. A. Gelston argues that *yussad* can mean "repair, restore" and not necessarily "to lay a foundation." But surely the repairing of the old foundation was involved initially. See 2 Ch 24:12-13, 27, and *Vetus Testamentum,* 16 (April 1966): 232-35.

terized conditions since the laying of the Temple foundation, but *from now on* things will change for the better.

The mention of the completion of the foundation constitutes both a promise and a warning. As a result of their renewed labors on the Temple, the people had the same potential blessing from God as they did back in 536 when the foundation was laid. If the work had not ground to a halt then, God would have blessed abundantly, even as He promises to do if they continue faithful in 520. Comforting are the Lord's words in verse 19: "I will bless" and not curse you. This time obedience is anticipated. Although the blessing is not described in terms as elaborate as Malachi 3:10, yet the same sharp contrast between curse and blessing is evident in both passages.

The first part of verse 19 probes the continuing effects of the curse on the people and the products of the land. True, they had turned to the Lord in the last few months, but no new harvest could be expected within that time. Sin can be forgiven while at the same time the consequences of that sin are still felt.

Using his final rhetorical question, Haggai asks how the supply of "seed" in the barn is holding out. "Seed" has the meaning of "yield" here, what the seed produces, as it does also in Leviticus 27:30 and Job 39:12. When applied to men, "seed" commonly refers to "offspring" or "descendants." The grain harvest took place from April to June, and six months later Haggai expects the answer to his question to be negative. The remains from the poor harvest were nil.

Then what about the summer fruit? Were the results any better? The Gezer Calendar, an inscription found in Palestine dating from around 900 BC, informs us that grapes, figs, and pomegranates were harvested in August and September, and olives from September to November. Even these more recent harvests had produced little fruit. The drought of 1:11 had taken its toll on the major products of the land. With the prospect of God's blessing, however, the people are challenged to match the faith of Habakkuk, who rejoiced in the Lord

> Though the fig tree should not blossom,
> And there be no fruit on the vines,
> Though the yield of the olive should fail,
> And the fields produce no food (Hab 3:17).

God Himself should be the source of our happiness, not just the things that He gives us.

5

Fourth Message

V. FOURTH MESSAGE: The Promise Concerning Zerubbabel (2:20-23)

THROUGHOUT THE BOOK, Governor Zerubbabel has been a key figure, leading the returned exiles in responding to God's word. The final few verses of the book tie Zerubbabel to important future events, as Haggai refers once more to shaking heaven and earth and the overthrow of nations (2:6-7).

A. The Overthrow of the Nations (2:20-22)

For the second time on that same twenty-fourth day of the ninth month, a message from God came to Haggai. This fourth and last revelation to the prophet brings the book to a climax as it explains how the blessing promised in verse 19 will eventually result in the political exaltation of Israel.

In contrast to the first two messages, the Lord directs His words only to Zerubbabel the governor. Joshua, the high priest, is not included. Verse 21 repeats the content of verse 6, shedding welcome light on "the shaking of heaven and earth." The relationship between verses 21 and 22 and verses 6-9 has already been analyzed in comments about the earlier passage. Here in the closing verses of the book, the outlook is more eschatological.

Verse 22 leaves little doubt that a complete collapse of the political power of the nations of the world lies in the offing. Using the word *overthrow,* often applied to the judgment upon Sodom and Gomorrah (e.g., Amos 4:11), God predicts that thrones will fall, along with their military capacity. Chariots and horses represent the epitome of strength for ancient warfare. Significantly, the word *power* or *strength* occurs in the verbal form rendered "take courage" in 2:4. If the Lord is the strength of our lives, our security surpasses that of the most powerful nations with all their weapons.

The collapse of the might of kingdoms will involve confusion and panic as they fall "every one by the sword of another." This fighting among themselves characterized the response of the Midianites to Gideon's surprise attack in Judges 7:22, and there are two eschatological passages which also employ the same idiom. One is Ezekiel 38:19-23, where the overthrow of God is described in terms close to Haggai 2. Not only is "every man's sword against his brother," but man and beast will *shake* before the presence of the God of judgment. The same Hebrew word appears in Haggai 2:21.

Another parallel is found in Zechariah 14:13-14, a passage dealing with the final battle of the nations against Jerusalem. God will overwhelm them with plague and panic, and, as a result, the gold, silver, and valuable garments of the nations will accrue to Israel. Earlier, in verses 7-9, Haggai had connected the shaking of the nations with the enriching of His house. Ultimately, this will be fulfilled as Christ returns to crush the nations and inaugurate His Kingdom.

B. The Exaltation of Zerubbabel (2:23)

In the final verse of the book, Haggai brings his message to a climax as he underscores the important position of Zerubbabel. It is impossible to separate the time designation "on that day" from the preceding verses, so the thought continues to be eschatological. But did the prophet actually expect Zerubbabel to be involved in heroics of Messianic proportions? Was the governor in fact to be identified with the Messiah?

Such claims would have brought Persian authorities on the run, but it is clear from the writing of Haggai's contemporary, Zechariah, that he was not being groomed as king of a vast domain. In Zechariah 6:11-13, we read of the symbolic crowning of Joshua, the high priest, who was a picture of the "Branch," the Messiah who would reign as Priest-King and build the Temple. If Haggai intended to attribute ruling powers to Zerubbabel, it would be strange to see Zechariah contradicting him so soon.

This is not to say, however, that Zerubbabel has no link with the Messiah, because the very terms used in verse 23 have Messianic import. Rather than bearing his usual title of "governor" (1:1, 14; 2:2, 21), Zerubbabel is called "my servant," a designation reserved for Christ, particularly in Isaiah (42:1; 52:13). The Lord also "chose" Zerubbabel, just as the Servant of Isaiah 42:1 is said to be a "chosen one."

Crucial to the understanding of this verse is the meaning of the "signet ring" to which Zerubbabel is being compared. The word could also be translated "seal," because a person's seal functioned as a signature in ancient times. The imprint of a king's seal on a letter validated the authority of the contents (1 Ki 21:8). A seal could also serve as a pledge or guarantee of future payment, as in the case of Judah and Tamar (Gen 38:18). This signet-seal was either worn on a finger of the right hand (Jer 22:24) or hung on a cord around the neck (Gen 38: 18). Song of Solomon 8:6 combines both methods, as it illustrates the preciousness of the seal.

Jeremiah 22:24 provides the key to the application of this figure to Zerubbabel, for in that passage his grandfather, King Jehoiachin (Coniah) is pulled off like a signet ring and cast into the hand of Nebuchadnezzar. In addition to exile in Babylon, Jehoiachin received the curse that none of his descendants would ever rule on David's throne (22:30). Yet in Matthew 1:12, Jeconiah (another name for Jehoiachin) appears in Christ's genealogy along with Zerubbabel.

Perhaps these passages can be reconciled through viewing Haggai 2:23 as a reinstatement of the family of Jehoiachin, a reversal of the curse pronounced in Jeremiah. Judges 17:2 illustrates the use of a blessing to cancel the effects of a curse. By making Zerubbabel a signet ring, Haggai may be saying that this Jewish leader is a pledge or guarantee that the Davidic dynasty will someday produce the Messiah.[14] The New Testament teaches that the Holy Spirit seals believers as a pledge, or down payment, guaranteeing our future inheritance (2 Co 1:22; Eph 1:13-14). Likewise, Zerubbabel validated the promise of the coming Messiah.

A further connection between Zerubbabel and Jeremiah 22 is seen in the meaning of his name: "descendant [or seed] of Babylon." It was the "descendants" of Jehoiachin who were banished to Babylon and who would not ascend his throne (22:28, 30). Yet it was a "seed of Babylon" who now represented the restoration of the Davidic promises. Zerubbabel was not the Messiah, but, like Christ, he led his people out of bondage and built a Temple.

That Temple had not been completed by the end of this short book, but important progress had been made. Haggai had powerfully motivated the people through the promises of God, so that the work was sure to be finished by an obedient Israel. What had appeared to be a remote possibility four months earlier, at the start of Haggai's ministry, was now almost a reality. Great changes can occur in the lives of individuals and nations when people turn to God in faith.

14. R. T. Siebeneck, "The Messianism of Aggeus and Proto-Zacharias," *Catholic Biblical Quarterly,* 19 (1957): 318.

MALACHI

6

Introduction to Malachi

Historical Background

As a result of the prophetic activity of Haggai and Zechariah, Zerubbabel was able to complete the Temple by 515 BC and usher in full-scale worship of the Lord. The new Temple was dedicated amid great rejoicing, and the festivals of the Lord were faithfully kept (Ezra 6:16-22). Nothing more is heard about the Judean community until the seventh year of King Artaxerxes (458 BC), when Ezra, the scribe, led another group of exiles back to Jerusalem. He was given financial resources by the Persians, who encouraged him to buy animals and other materials and bring sacrifices and offerings to the Temple altar (Ezra 7:1-17). Ezra also taught the Law of Moses to the people and spearheaded a reform aimed against mixed marriages with surrounding nations.

In the twentieth year of Artaxerxes, 445 BC, a high-ranking official of the Persian government, Nehemiah, received permission to journey to Jerusalem and lead his people in rebuilding the walls of Jerusalem. This important task was completed in fifty-two days (Neh 6:15) under the vigorous oversight of this newly appointed governor. Nehemiah also instituted financial reforms to protect the poor (Neh 5:2-13) and signed an agreement, along with other leaders, promising to avoid mixed marriages, to keep the Sabbath, and to contribute annually to the

Temple a third of a shekel of silver. In addition, the agreement provided for the bringing of tithes and firstfruits for the support of the Levites and the Temple worship (Neh 10).

After completing his twelve-year stint in Jerusalem, Nehemiah returned to the Persian king, and during his absence, the people violated almost all the terms of this agreement (Neh 13:6). The tithes were not given, the Sabbath was disregarded, intermarriage was rampant, and the priests became corrupt (Neh 13:7-31). Such widespread iniquity must have consumed several years before Nehemiah was once again able to secure permission to travel to Jerusalem and rectify the situation—with a vengeance.[1] It was precisely the sins dealt with by Nehemiah which Malachi condemned (1:6-14; 2:14-16; 3:8-11), making it likely that the prophet worked in conjunction with the governor. Malachi's firm rebuke of spiritual and moral corruption sounds a note urgently needed in our own day.

Date. The correspondence between the list of sins in Nehemiah 13 and those against which Malachi preached suggests a date during Nehemiah's second period as governor or just prior to his return. This hinges on the meaning of the term *governor* in Malachi 1:8, where it is felt that Nehemiah might have been mentioned by name if he were the ruling governor. Certainly Haggai refers specifically to Zerubbabel several times in his short book, and it is difficult to explain Malachi's total lack of reference to the godly Nehemiah if he was residing in Jerusalem. Moreover, the tone of 1:8 implies that a heathen governor would not be treated as badly as their own God.

If, however, the governor was someone other than Nehemiah, his name has not been preserved for us in any historical record. There is also the fact that, after his indeterminate stay with Artaxerxes, Nehemiah returned to take immediate and full control (Neh 13:9-11, 19, 21) in Judah. Yet the length of his absence might have necessitated the rule of an intervening governor.

1. C. F. Keil, *The Books of Ezra, Nehemiah, and Esther* (Grand Rapids: Eerdmans, 1949), p. 149. A thorough discussion of the length of Nehemiah's absence from Judah.

Some suggest that the term for "governor," employed in verse 8 (*pehah*), indicates a foreign personage. While it is true that Nehemiah is usually called *"tirshatha,"* a Persian title for governor (Neh 10:1), the word *pehah* is also attributed to Nehemiah in 5:14. This alternative designation for "governor" is derived from Assyrian official language, and it is repeatedly applied to Governor Zerubbabel in Haggai (1:1, 14). Hence, one cannot automatically eliminate Nehemiah from consideration in Malachi 1:8, especially when one compares the respect for this governor with the stern actions of Nehemiah in driving out foreigners with their goods and demanding of the Jews obedience to the Law (Neh 13:8, 11, 25, 28).

If Malachi prophesied during Nehemiah's second stay in Jerusalem, his ministry would have paralleled the relationship of Haggai and Zechariah to the earlier governor, Zerubbabel. Both Haggai and Zechariah ministered more than fifteen years after Zerubbabel's coming to Jerusalem, and it is likely that a comparable time span is involved in the case of Malachi and Nehemiah. This would tentatively place the ministry of Malachi after 433, perhaps beginning before the controversial return of Nehemiah to Judah.

The prophet. Nothing is known about the family background or the life of Malachi, outside the pages of his short book. There is even doubt as to whether "Malachi" is a proper name. The word occurs in 3:1, meaning "my messenger" or "my angel," and it is also found without the possessive suffix in 2:7 and 3:1. Since it is an important concept in the book, could this have been selected as a title for the whole prophecy, without regard to the actual name of the prophet? The Septuagint handles verse 1 as "by the hand of his messenger," and other tradition ties the book to "my messenger, Ezra."

Yet it would be very strange indeed if the Hebrews preserved a prophetic book without giving the name of the author. Even as short a book as Obadiah does not lack the name of the inspired writer, although nothing else is known about him. Many Hebrew names end in *i*, like Malachi, and sometimes this is an abbreviation for the divine name "Yah" or "Yahweh" (i.e., Jehovah). As a proper noun, "Malachi" (short for "Malachiyah") would mean "messenger of Yahweh" (see 2:7), a most fitting name for one who penned important words about several key messengers.

Style. The book of Malachi exhibits more of a poetic flair than Haggai, and there are some who attempt to arrange the whole book in poetic lines. Parallelism can be discerned in several verses, but it is not the consistent balancing of words and thoughts that characterizes true Hebrew poetry. Perhaps "lofty prose" is still the best way to describe the style of Malachi.

The most striking feature in the book is the running dialogue between a righteous God and a sarcastic, unfaithful people. Much of this interchange is punctuated with questions, both from God and the people (1:2, 6, 7, 8, 9, 13; 2:10, 14, 15, 17; 3:2, 7, 8, 13). Once in Haggai (1:2) the people were quoted and then answered by an aroused God; but frequently in Malachi the expression "you say" is given, followed by God's resounding answers (1:2, 6, 7, 12, 13; 2:14, 17; 3:7, 8, 13). The people were saying that they were innocent of God's charges or that serving God was useless, while God was replying that His allegations were completely true and that He deserved far greater respect. The careless attitude of the people is clearly portrayed through their own flippant words.

Malachi's skillful use of questions reminds one of the technique of Habakkuk in his short prophecy almost two hundred years earlier. Habakkuk himself addressed a series of questions to God, and the Lord answered each one. In Malachi, however, the interrogative method is expanded even further.

Repetition of words and figures of speech also marks the style of the book. Twenty times within the fifty-five verses, the notation "says the LORD of hosts" appears. Variations of the expression add to the claim of the prophet that he possessed the very words of God.

The greatness of the name of God (1:5, 11, 14; 2:2) is contrasted to the lack of respect on the part of the people (1:6, 12; 2:13-14). God was seeking those who would fear (revere, respect) Him, and this idea is reiterated throughout the book (1:6, 11, 14; 2:5; 3:5, 16; 4:2, 5). For those who genuinely fear Him, God would guarantee future glory, but judgment awaited those who denied and neglected His warnings.

Another recurring contrast is that between love and hate. God proved His love to Israel (1:2) and would continue to love them (3:17), whereas Israel was involved in polluting God's sanctuary (1:12-13) and in treacherous actions against Him (2:10-11). God desired to bless His people abundantly (2:2; 3:10), but their wayward behavior forced Him to curse them repeatedly (1:14; 2:2; 3:9; 4:6).

On occasion, Malachi employs a figure of speech and then develops the same figure in a later passage. The "rising of the sun" (1:11) imagery is expanded in the "sun of righteousness" in 4:2. Similarly, the refiner's fire (3:2) is to be related to the "burning like a furnace" in 4:1. These are vivid figures, appropriate to the powerful and frank expression of the Lord's prophet.

Outline of Malachi

I. God's Love for Israel (1:1-5)
   A. The Heading (1:1)
   B. God's Love Questioned (1:2a)
   C. God's Love for Israel and Edom Contrasted (1:2b-4)
   D. God's Greatness in View (1:5)

II. The Unfaithfulness of the Priests (1:6—2:9)
   A. The Priests Pollute the Sanctuary (1:6-14)
      1. They dishonor the Lord (1:6)
      2. They offer unacceptable sacrifices (1:7-10)
      3. They deny the greatness of God's name (1:11-14)

7

God Confronts Israel

I. GOD'S LOVE FOR ISRAEL (1:1-5)

NO OTHER NATION was privileged to have Israel's position before God. They were uniquely related to Him, bound by a solemn covenant made on Mt. Sinai. The descendants of Abraham and Jacob were singled out as people of a special destiny, and it seems strange to find God having to prove His love to Israel.

A. The Heading (1:1)

God's message to Israel is introduced as "the oracle of the word of the LORD." The combining of "oracle" with "the word of the LORD" also occurs in Zechariah 9:1 and 12:1, a fact that has led some critics to regard these three concluding sections of the Old Testament as anonymous appendages to the minor prophets. Since the number twelve is symbolic of the twelve tribes, they theorize that this last of the three oracles, "Malachi," was artificially separated from the others to arrive at a total of twelve minor prophets. Such reasoning is not convincing, except to show that the expression "oracle of the word of the LORD" was used exclusively after the Babylonian exile.

"Oracle" does occur as a heading several other times (Is 13:1; 14:28; Nah 1:1; Hab 1:1). It could also be translated "burden," which reflects the verb *to lift up, carry,* from which it is derived. Usually "oracle" or "burden" introduces a divine declaration of a threatening nature, although promises can be included in the message. This leads some commentators to regard it as a synonym for "prophecy" or "proclamation."[2] The idea of a threat

2. Theodore Laetsch, *The Minor Prophets,* pp. 293-94.

does suit the purpose of Malachi, however, for some stern words of judgment were involved. A good modern equivalent for "oracle, burden" is the expression young people sometimes use about the Scriptures. They refer to a meaningful passage as "heavy"; it is an important word from God to them, and this idiom is close to the biblical term.

God's word came "through" Malachi, literally, "by the hand of," or, "by the agency of" Malachi. Often this preposition is used of God's communicating His word through prophets, Moses in particular (Ex 9:35). Haggai 1:1 employs the same terminology with reference to "the prophet Haggai." Since "through, by means of" is normally followed by the name of the prophet, the interpretation of "Malachi" as a proper name rather than as a common noun is strengthened.

B. God's Love Questioned (1:2a)

With characteristic abruptness, Malachi launches into his message as he relates God's wonderful words to Israel: "I have loved you." Down through centuries of varied experience, God has displayed His love and compassion for this one nation in countless ways. He entered a marriage relationship with them as a faithful Husband (Eze 16:1-15), only to see the people spurn His love. He had freed them from the prison of Egypt and led them into a fertile country, but Israel had rejected Him. Yet He, the unchangeable One (Mal 3:6), did not reject them. In fact, His love remained steady, and verse 2 could equally well be translated, "I love you." It was the deep love of a husband for a wife (2:11) or of a father for a son (1:6; 3:17), and it had been proved time and time again. Though Israel's sin made exile necessary, God had graciously brought them back home again.

So it is surprising to hear the response to God's true statement of love: "How hast Thou loved us?" What is the evidence that You really have loved us? This shocking reply sets the tone for the entire book, as assertion after assertion is challenged by an ungrateful nation. How quickly men can forget God's wondrous actions of kindness on their behalf! (Ps 78:9-17).

C. God's Love for Israel and Edom Contrasted (1:2b-4)

To support His claim of love, God refers to the respective conditions of the nations descended from the twin brothers, Jacob and Esau. Both were the sons of the chosen Isaac, though Esau was the firstborn. Yet, with a deft question, God introduces the obvious contrast between the two. Edom, the nation of Esau, lay in ruins, facing the perpetual indignation of God.

The difference between the two countries is expressed as God loving Jacob and hating Esau. The meaning of God's hatred has perplexed and confused many, but a solution is readily available from Scripture. In Genesis 29:30-33, a close parallel is found in the status of Jacob's two wives, Rachel and Leah. Verse 30 states that Jacob loved Rachel more than Leah, while verses 31 and 33 describe Leah as "hated." She was "hated" in the sense that she came out second best in her rivalry with Rachel, so the New American Standard Bible is correct in translating the word "unloved" rather than "hated."

Deuteronomy 21:15-17 also deals with the problem of two wives who are not loved equally.

In the New Testament the same modified use of "hate" occurs in the passage about hating one's own parents or family in order to follow Christ (Lk 14:26). This is explained in Matthew 10:37 as a matter of loving God *more than* parents or family. Only in that sense can it be called "hatred."

Paul, in Romans 9:10-15, relates this "loving" and "hating" to God's choice of Jacob before the two were born. God's sovereign purpose was at work here, but it is also true that Esau became an "immoral" and "godless" person deserving of his fate (Heb 12:16). Jacob, the "supplanter," was equally unworthy of God's love, yet received the inheritance with all its blessings. And under the disciplining hand of God, "Jacob" became "Israel," a prince with God.

Meanwhile, Esau's inheritance had become a desolation, a playground for jackals. The terminology in verses 3-4 is closely related to passages in Jeremiah (as in 9:11), and it may be that Malachi is describing the fall of Edom in terms that the weeping prophet had used for Israel itself. The word for "beaten down" or "demolished" occurs only in verse 4 and in Jeremiah 5:17. Likewise, the ideas of "building" and "tearing down" reflect the keynote of Jeremiah's message (Jer 1:10). Of necessity God had to tear down Israel, but He promised to rebuild their cities. For Edom there would be no rebuilding.

The destruction of Edom is sometimes considered to be the work of Nebuchadnezzar, who devastated Judah and attacked some surrounding nations in his 587 BC campaigns. More likely, however, the collapse of Edom to which Malachi is referring was the work of the Nabataean Arabs, who drove out the Edomites between 550 and 400 BC. The Nabataeans developed into a powerful kingdom that included Transjordan, and they endured until the Romans conquered them at about AD 100. Meanwhile the Edomites were forced to settle in southern Palestine in a region called Idumea.[3] Since the Nabataean invasion was roughly contemporary with Malachi, the illustration was an apt one.

Edom desired to regain possession of their homeland and to rebuild the ruins, but this desire was never fulfilled. Instead, Edom was known as "the wicked territory" because of the sin that characterized their national life and that brought God's judgment upon them. Israel had felt the indignation of God's wrath at the collapse of Jerusalem (Lam 2:6), but this indignation would last only a little while (cf. Is 10:25). Edom, however, would experience God's indignation perpetually.

D. God's Greatness in View (1:5)

As Israel observes the plight of brother Esau, he will be forced to admit that God has intervened and has indeed demonstrated His love for Israel. This conclusion will be inescapable, a fact

3. Laetsch, p. 209.

the prophet stresses through the emphatic *"your eyes* will see this and *you* will say." At no time since the birth of Jacob and Esau has evidence of God's love for Jacob been lacking.

The exact meaning of the people's response is disputed. Will they say, "The LORD is great beyond the border of Israel," or, "The LORD be magnified above the border of Israel"? Both interpretations have their supporters, and both are possible, but the first rendering seems better. God's great acts are evident within the territory of Israel but also above and beyond the borders of the chosen land. Verses 11 and 14 elaborate upon the greatness of God, and each verse refers to God's being great among the nations. Judgment upon a Pharaoh or upon Edom compels them to acknowledge that Israel's God is the true God, but somehow the Lord's own people are slow to recognize His mighty works on their behalf.

8

The Failures of the Priests

II. THE UNFAITHFULNESS OF THE PRIESTS (1:6—2:9)

A. The Priests Pollute the Sanctuary (1:6-14)

GOD'S LOVE FOR ISRAEL is sharply contrasted with the loveless attitude displayed toward Him by the nation. Oddly, it was the priests who, in spite of their sacred privileges as God's ministers, led the way in showing lack of respect.

1. *They Dishonor the Lord* (1:6)

Having successfully defended the assertion concerning His love, the Lord moves to a second topic in verse 6. His love for them has been great, so He expects the honor that a son gives his father or the respect a servant gives his master. Such a response to natural parents was specified in the Ten Commandments, and if one's father was God, the honor should have been even greater

The Lord had specifically selected Israel as His son (Jer 31:9), and the nation was equally well known as the servant of the Lord (Is 42:19). In fact, the word *master,* while used occasionally of human masters (Ex 21:4), is normally the word translated "Lord" ("LORD" equals "Jehovah" or "Yahweh") throughout the New American Standard Bible. In Malachi it appears also in 1:12 and in 3:1.

As a highly favored son and servant, Israel had every reason to display the greatest respect for God. But God's questions bare the sad truth: "Where is My honor? Where is My respect?" It was strangely lacking. The word *honor* is the same word often translated "glory," and this adds to the irony. The great and glorious God, Creator of heaven and earth, is deprived of what little "glory" or "honor" Israel could render to Him. In Haggai 1:8, an earlier generation was challenged to rebuild the Temple and glorify God, and here in Malachi, God's glory is again related to the Temple. "Respect" may be too mild a rendering, since the concept involves "fear" or "dread" and is derived from the verb *to fear, revere,* which occurs repeatedly in Malachi. God is looking for those whose attitudes and actions display a reverent awe for Him.

One would think that the priests, who performed the sacrifices and guarded the Law, would best exemplify such behavior, but the Lord singles them out as major violators. Unlike their ancestors, who had profound respect for God's name (2:5), the priests were guilty of despising God's name. Whether consciously or subconsciously, the religious leaders were not only failing to honor God, they actually showed contempt for His name. This is a serious charge and is immediately challenged. "How have we despised Thy name?" In verse 2 they asked for proof that God loved them; now in verse 6 they request evidence that they have spurned God.

The shocking attitude of this son-servant is also discussed by Isaiah at the start of his lengthy prophecy. In Isaiah 1:2-3, God complains that His sons have turned out to be rebels. An ox or a donkey knows its owner and where it is fed, but the people of Israel refuse to acknowledge that God is their sustainer. The imagery in both passages is remarkably similar.

2. They Offer Unacceptable Sacrifices (1:7-10)

a. The Nature of the Sacrifices (1:7-8a). The proof that Israel and the priests in particular were disrespectful to God was most obvious in the way they handled the sacrificial system. There were flagrant violations of the code laid down in Leviticus. It would seem logical that after Haggai and Zechariah had successfully motivated the people to rebuild the Temple, proper worship would follow naturally, but it proved easier to complete God's house than to live in it for His glory.

God's name was being despised because the priests were presenting defiled food upon His altar. The Hebrew word order, by placing "upon My altar" before "defiled food," reveals the nerve of these priests. You dare to do this to *My* sacred altar! "Food" or "bread" is a way of referring to the offerings presented to God (Lev 21:6), though this has no connection with the pagan idea that the gods depended on sacrifices for their daily sustenance.

The food is called "polluted" or "contaminated," a term usually referring to hands or clothes stained with blood (Is 59:3; 63:3; Lam 4:14). This makes the individuals "unclean" and unfit for contact with anything sacred. Bloody sacrifices were designed to atone for sin, but in the hands of these priests, the blood succeeded only in polluting the sacrifices and the altar.

The priests' reply to the charge of presenting defiled food is hard to follow. Why do they ask, "How have we defiled Thee?" rather than, "How is the food defiled?" Perhaps they are admitting that the offerings were polluted while at the same time differentiating between God and His altar. God's answer indicates that He may be hurt more by their whole attitude toward His table than by the unacceptable sacrifices offered there.

This attitude considers the Lord's table despicable, worthless. Serving the Lord was a lowly, miserable job which they clearly despised. *Despicable* is a strong term, used also in Daniel 11:21 to describe Antiochus Epiphanes, the Syrian king who sacrificed a pig on this same Temple altar in Jerusalem and tried to exterminate Judaism about 165 BC. Such actions on the part of a pagan ruler may be understandable, but how can the very priests of the Lord in any way share this contempt?

Malachi employs the word *table* in place of "altar," a usage also found in Ezekiel 44:16. Normally the table was distinguished from the altar, since the showbread or "bread of the Presence" was placed on the table in the holy place. *Table* may be used because "bread" replaces "offerings" earlier in this verse. Bread on a table suggests fellowship with God more than a sacrifice on an altar, and Malachi is explaining that this fellowship has been badly disrupted.

Verse 8 specifies exactly why the sacrifices are polluted: because the priests are offering blind and lame animals. According to Deuteronomy 15:21, animals with serious blemishes of any kind were unacceptable as sacrifices, and blindness and lameness are mentioned in particular. The word translated "serious" in Deuteronomy 15:21 is the same one rendered "evil" here in verse 8. Rather than "Is it not evil?" being a question, the Lord is probably quoting the people. As they presented defective sacrifices, they said, or at least thought, "There's nothing wrong with that; it isn't serious. God will be happy with it."

b. *The Response to These Sacrifices* (1:8a-10). In reply the Lord challenges them to try *that* to impress their governor. What would *he* think of such pitiful gifts? Could you expect any favors after such disgraceful behavior? No animals like that would be acceptable as payment of any debts, and obviously no one would dare to insult the governor in this way.

Both the terms *be pleased with* and *receive you kindly* are used with reference to sacrifices to God, but they also occur on the human level. When Jacob sought to atone for his earlier behavior against Esau, he brought a large number of animals as a present, in the hope that Esau would accept him (Gen 32:20; 33:10). This expression is literally, "to lift up the face," for Jacob bowed to the ground before his estranged brother. One who "lifts up your face" shows a high regard for you and is willing to grant your request (see 1 Sa 25:35).

Continuing in an ironic vein, the Lord asks the disrespectful priests to pray on behalf of "us," the people. The word *entreat* is actually "to weaken, soften up" the face of God; it is related to the word *sick* or *weak* in verse 8, as Malachi uses a play on words. If you would not dare to treat the governor in this way, try softening up *God* to gain His favor!

In Exodus 32:11 Moses attempted to placate an angry God intent on destroying Israel. Would the priests of Malachi's time in their wicked condition, try to intercede successfully for the people? Absurd! Because of their attitude and the kind of sacrifice they were bringing, God was certain to deny their every request.

In New Testament terms, God is seeking living sacrifices that will be holy and acceptable to Him (Ro 12:1-2; cf. comments on Hag 1:8). All too often, Christians feel that anything is good enough for God. As long as a person or an activity is even half-heartedly dedicated to God, we assume God will be delighted with us. So the Church limps along with unanswered prayers and lack of power because we do not take God's standards seriously. Whatever we do should be done for the glory of God, who deserves the very best we can offer (1 Co 10:31).

To make sure that His feelings are crystal clear, the Lord abandons the use of rhetorical questions and speaks directly in verse 10. He expresses the strange wish that someone would close the doors of the Temple and bring a sharp halt to the offering of sacrifices. While some might question such drastic action, it was nonetheless obvious that "kindling fires" on His altar was useless, since unfit priests were bringing unfit sacrifices. God finds no satisfaction in such offerings or the people who bring them.

Closing the doors is equivalent to locking them. In Israel's past, the Temple doors had been locked with dire consequences. Wicked King Ahaz had terminated the Temple worship as he made altars in every corner of Jerusalem (2 Ch 28:24). His pagan ideas only hastened the downfall of Judah. Yet God Himself had gone on record as being "fed up" with empty worship. In Isaiah 1:13 the Lord thundered, "Bring your worthless offerings no longer," for the people were steeped in sin and wickedness of every kind. Their activity in the Temple was received as the "trampling of My courts" (Is 1:12). God had effectively closed the doors of Solomon's Temple with the Babylonian destruction of Jerusalem, and the Roman armies would do the same to Zerubbabel's and Herod's Temple in AD 70.

On the modern scene, there is nothing automatically praiseworthy about opening the church doors every Sunday. Going through the motions of an empty ritual will not please God any more than the perverted worship of Malachi's contemporaries. One wonders how many churches deserve to stay open, based on the genuine worship and education carried on within their doors. I have heard of one evangelical church which has gone thirty-five years without seeing one young person embark on a career in some phase of Christian service. How does God react to that kind of fruitlessness?

3. They Deny the Greatness of God's Name (1:11-14)

a. God's Name Great Among the Nations (1:11). The disrespectful attitude of the Jewish priests stands in sharp contrast to the nations of the world, who acknowledge that God is indeed great. Verse 11 describes the worldwide influence of Israel's God, but it is a passage with such great implications that it has received varied interpretations. When will God's name be great among the nations, and how literal will these new Jerusalem offerings be?

Most translations supply "will be" twice in the verse to indicate that they feel this verse can only apply to the future, when Christ appears on the scene and the Gospel is made available to the Gentiles. This futuristic interpretation is probably the most popular one, but it is also true that in some sense God's name was great among the nations even in Malachi's day.

Instead of supplying "will be" in the verse, it is, in fact, preferable to translate "My name is great among the nations." Support for the present tense is found in verses 5 and 14, particularly the latter, where "I am a great King," and, "My name is feared among the nations," are clearly applicable to Malachi's own time (see comments on 1:5). These expressions are so close to the one in verse 11 that some present meaning must be found there also.

In verse 5 God's greatness was seen historically in His judgment against Edom, and it is this same judging work against the
nations which probably accounts for the respect shown to the
Lord in verse 11. Zephaniah 2:11 provides an important parallel
to Malachi 1:11, for it describes Israel's awesome God as He
judges nations such as Moab, Assyria, and Ethiopia, showing
the impotency of their gods. Humbled by the Lord, "The nations
will bow down to Him, every one from his own place." The ideas
of God's greatness and of worship from "every place" correspond
closely to key thoughts in Malachi 1:11.

Malachi, however, seems to imply more than a grudging ac-
knowledgment of the greatness of God on the part of Gentiles.
Is it possible that God's mighty acts have led some Gentiles to
genuine faith in the Lord? Nineveh had responded in large numbers to the preaching of Jonah in the eighth century BC, and other
Gentiles are numbered among Old Testament believers. Using
terminology similar to verse 11, Isaiah speaks of God's raising
up Cyrus to conquer Babylon and release Israel from captivity,
"That men may know from the rising to the setting of the sun
That there is no one besides Me" (Is 45:6). This "knowledge"
could mean a saving relationship for some individuals.

A major problem with this interpretation is Malachi's reference to incense and offerings. Could non-Jews offer legitimate
sacrifices to God in a place other than Jerusalem? This is hard to
prove, unless the case of Job applies. Yet one could argue that
these offerings are to be understood as "the freewill offerings" of
one's mouth (Ps 119:108); "the meditation of my heart," which,
like any other sacrifice, can be "acceptable in Thy sight" (Ps
19:14; Heb 13:15). The word translated "grain offering" can
also mean the tribute paid by one nation to another (Ho 10:6),
although such payments are not elsewhere described as "pure."
"Incense" strongly reflects worship on a literal altar, though this
particular word for "incense" does not occur again in the Old
Testament. Revelation 5:8, however, does connect incense with
the prayers of the saints.

The major thrust of the verse is that the Gentiles, who did not have the benefit of the clarity of God's revelation to the Jews, are honoring the Lord more than the Jews. The entrance of the Gentiles into the place of blessing is of course more prominent in the New Testament, so the verse does apply legitimately to the future.

At the conversion of the Gentile Cornelius, Peter unmistakably refers to this verse in saying, "The man who fears Him and does what is right, is welcome [acceptable] to Him" (Ac 10:35). A verse earlier, Peter states that God does not show partiality, a thought also reflected in Malachi 2:9 (see also 3:14-16). The name and reputation of God earned the respect and worship of nations in the past, and it will become increasingly clear in the future that the Lord is the true God. Someday every knee will bow before Him (Phil 2:10).

Ultimately, the fulfillment of this verse is to be found in the worldwide rule of Christ, when the Gentiles will bring offerings to Jerusalem from the ends of the earth. The wealth of the nations will be turned over to Israel (Is 60:5-9), and the Jews themselves are said to be brought back to Israel as a kind of "offering" to the Lord (Is 66:20). Significantly, Malachi 1:11 could be translated "from every place," rather than, "in every place," an interpretation that would correspond nicely to the millennial offerings brought from all over the world.[4] This would ease the problem of having legitimate places of worship outside Jerusalem itself.

b. God's Name Disdained by the Priests (1:12-14). Verses 12-14 expand the condemnation of the priests and their activities, which was started in verses 6-10. Compared with the pure worship of the Lord, outlined in verse 11, their attitudes and behavior are even more reprehensible. The twelfth verse is a restatement of verse 7, although it does introduce a word for "pollute, profane" not used earlier. This term stands in stark

4. Another example of "in" meaning "from" is found in Isaiah 21:1, "from the Negev." See E. J. Young, *The Book of Isaiah* (Grand Rapids: Eerdmans, 1969), 2:60.

contrast to verse 11. There, God's name was regarded as great
among the nations, but you—the priests of the Lord—are profaning it! In Leviticus 21:6-7, the priests are forbidden to profane God's name by coming in contact with dead bodies or
marrying anyone other than a virgin. They have a holy task and
must be set apart to God. But since they are defiling His sanctuary, they are indeed profaning the Lord's holy name (Lev
20:3).

Specifically, God charges that they are treating His name as
common, because they say, or at least think, "The table of the
Lord is defiled." This is almost identical to their statement in
verse 7, except that "defiled" replaces "despised." Those who
despise the Lord's table are certain to defile it. In fact, they
regard the fruit or food, the sacrifices themselves, as despicable.
The priests received part of most offerings presented to the Lord
as their own food, and they may be complaining about the quality
of these meals. The best parts of these maimed sacrifices belonged to the Lord, and what was left was none too good. If the
priests had insisted that the people bring healthy animals, this
sad situation would not have existed.

On the other hand, in light of verses 7 and 13, the "despicable
food" seems more directly applicable to what is offered to God.
The whole sacrificial system has become to the priests a tiresome
chore instead of participation in the glorious ministry of the Almighty God. They are treating this holy service with contempt
and are actually sneering at it as one would scoff at his enemies
(Ps 10:5).

Isaiah spoke about Israel as tired of God and not willing to
offer any sacrifices to Him (Is 43:22-24). The same passage
says that they have wearied God with their sins, and the priests
had certainly exhausted the patience of God with their pitiful
sacrifices (cf. Is 7:13). God was the One who deserved to be
disgusted with their behavior and to let loose His wrath with
an angry blast. This "sneering" of the Lord is indeed unleashed
in Malachi 3:2-3 (see Eze 22:21 and the comments on Hag 1:9).

Verse 8 mentions sacrificial "candidates" that were blind, lame, and sick; verse 13 includes the latter two along with specimens taken by robbery. Some had turned to stealing in order to bring God a pleasing offering, thereby compounding the guilt! Through Isaiah, the Lord had said, "I hate robbery in the burnt offering" (61:8), perhaps referring to this very practice. Several times this word for rob is linked to the oppression of widows and orphans (Job 24:2; Is 10:2). Robbing the poor and needy is hardly the way to gain God's favor. Any kind of a sacrifice that costs nothing is in reality no sacrifice at all. Chapter 3 describes this activity as robbing God (vv. 8-10).

In verse 13, using the same words as in verse 10, though this time in question form, the Lord asks, "Should I receive that from your hand?" Emphatically not. *That* kind of sacrifice is totally unacceptable, so why bring it?

The attitude of the priests has affected the entire populace, and verse 14 records the efforts of one wily individual to present a particularly deceptive sacrifice. The case concerns an offering in fulfillment of a vow, which, according to Leviticus 22:17-25, must be a male animal with no defect. Animals with certain deformities were acceptable as freewill offerings, but not to fulfill a vow (22:23). The man in question did have a male in his flock which he vowed to present to the Lord, but when the time came, he offered instead an animal with a defect. Rather than a blessing, his actions earned him the curse of the Lord, and he would have to suffer the consequences.

Since the man is called a "trickster" or "crafty conniver" (see Gen 37:18; Num 25:18), it is likely that he planned from the start to substitute the deformed animal. Vows were voluntary, but he wanted to be known as a spiritual individual. People would hear about him, because vows were usually fulfilled in public and the people might not notice the defective sacrifice. The fact that the priests were lax, however, was no excuse for anyone to present a polluted offering. God knew about the hypocrisy, even if no one else exposed him. The attempt of Ananias and Sapphira to present to God less than the whole price promised is a New Testament example of the same kind of hypocrisy (Ac 5:1-5).

The word for "blemished animal" is literally, "corruption," a term also used in the Leviticus parallel (Lev 22:25). The same expression appears in Isaiah 52:14, referring to the appearance of Christ in His sacrificial death. He was "marred" or "disfigured" to an astonishing extent as He bore the sin of the world. How ironic that a term normally reserved for unacceptable sacrifices describes the one Sacrifice that really atoned for sin. The awful effects of sin are visible in all of their horror.

Why is it such a terrible thing to bring defective sacrifices out of the wrong motives? It is because God is a great King whose name commands the respect of the nations. Returning to a theme already introduced in verses 5 and 11, Malachi uses in verse 14 a title claimed by some of the most powerful of earthly monarchs. The "great King" refers in 2 Kings 18:19, 28 to Sennacherib, the Assyrian ruler whose armies terrorized the Near East around 700 BC. And yet Israel's Lord, "a great God, And a great King above all gods" (Ps 95:3), saved Jerusalem from the grasp of that Assyrian monarch by destroying his unstoppable army.

In verse 8, Malachi contrasts their respect for God with their behavior before the governor. If the people shied away from insulting the governor, would they dare to defy the great Persian king who had appointed that governor? With far greater awe should they have been anxious to please the One who regards the nations as "a drop in the bucket" and who "reduces rulers to nothing" (Is 40:15, 23).

B. The Priests Cursed for Corrupting the Teaching of Levi (2:1-9)

1. *Priestly Neglect Brings God's Curse* (2:1-3)

Since the priests dishonored the Lord by polluting the sanctuary, severe punishment is in store for them. The dire warning given to them is called "this commandment" in verse 1. It is not

so much a "commandment" as it is a "decree" or a "resolution."
Nahum 1:14 provides another example of a "command" which
announces coming catastrophe. There, the judgment is directed
against the ungodly Assyrians, while in Malachi, strangely
enough, the priests of the Lord are the targets of His wrath.

As if to give His ministers another chance, God introduces the
punishment with a hopeful condition. Only if you do not respond
by honoring My name will this curse strike you. Yet, before the
verse is completed, the Lord is forced to admit that the priests are
in fact not responding and that He will have to carry out His
threat.

The Lord pleads with the priests to listen and to "place on the
heart" His words. This idiom is close to the English expression
to "take it to heart," that is, to take something seriously. It means
that one is aware of the facts and is willing to take appropriate
action to avoid a dangerous situation (see Is 42:25). In this
case, the action involves showing respect for the holy name of
the Lord, as Malachi uses the phrase "My name" for the sixth
time in sixteen verses (see comments on 1:6 also).

Unless wholehearted repentance takes place, God will have to
unleash the curse against the priests, and He will curse their
blessings. Sadly, this is exactly what happened, and those set
apart as sacred ministers of God found themselves cursed along
with the scheming conniver described in 1:14.

The priests were assigned the high privilege of pronouncing
blessings upon the people. It was their prerogative to invoke
"My name" and repeat the gracious words of Numbers 6:24-26,
so that the Lord would bless and keep the children of Israel and
give them peace. But now God was going to make these blessings
ineffective and bring about the exact opposite of what was
desired.

In Judges 17:2, a mother tried to reverse a horrible curse she
had uttered unknowingly against her own son, who confessed
stealing pieces of silver from her. She pronounced him blessed,
thereby releasing him from the dreaded curse. For the priests of

Malachi's day, this "reversal" would go the other way. Their words would speak of blessing, but God would turn them into a curse.

Frequently the idea of "curse" is associated in Scripture with famine and sterility, and verses 2-3 allude to this quite directly. First, the expression, "I will send the curse upon you" is almost a quotation from Deuteronomy 28:20, a passage that warns of famine, pestilence, and disease as consequences of sins. Earlier in this commentary, we noted extensive references to this very chapter in Haggai 1:6, 10-11, and 2:17.

A second factor linking Malachi 2:2-3 with Deuteronomy 28:20 is the word *rebuke,* found as a verb in the former passage and a noun in the latter. The word is the same, however, and this helps clarify the difficult clause in which it appears in verse 3. Literally, the Lord announces that He will "rebuke your seed." "Seed" is often correctly translated "offspring," but the connection with Deuteronomy 28 makes it more likely that the produce of the ground is intended. Malachi 3:9-11 mentions a curse which will be ended when the Lord will "rebuke the devourer for you" so that the crops will not be destroyed.

Deuteronomy 28:38 specifically refers to planting abundant seed only to have the locust devour it. In the curse section of Leviticus 26, God warns that they will sow seed uselessly, because their enemies will consume the harvest (Lev 26:15-16). How different from the situation described in Leviticus 25:21, where the Lord will "so order His blessing" that the crops just before the sabbatical year will last for three years.

Another factor in favor of interpreting "seed" in the sense of "produce" rather than "people" can be seen from a literal rendering of verse 3: "I am going to rebuke the seed for you." This may mean, not that God would rebuke "your seed," but that He would rebuke the seed "because of you."[5] Everyone's "seed" or "crops" would be affected by the gross sin of the priests. The

5. The use of the preposition *for* in a causal sense is illustrated twice in Gen 4:23.

individuals who were normally involved in blessing the people have become the cause for a curse upon the entire land.

To show the disgrace that will come to the priests, the Lord speaks of spreading refuse on their faces, even the refuse of their feasts. "Refuse" is perhaps better translated "entrails," because it was "the insides" of a sacrificial animal that were burned outside the camp along with the hide and flesh (Ex 29:14; Lev 8:17; 16:27). Usually it has reference to a bull used for a sin offering, so the Lord is throwing back in their faces the sad remains of what was supposed to be a sacred offering. In their condition, and in view of the defective animals offered, the whole sacrifice was held in contempt by the Lord.

The last line of verse 3 most likely means that the priests will suffer the same fate as the entrails or refuse. Just as these parts of the animal were taken outside the camp and burned, so the guilty priests would be separated from the community and destroyed. A similar coarse figure is applied to the descendants of King Jeroboam in 1 Kings 14:10. The family of that wicked king was to be destroyed as one burns up dung until it is all gone.

2. Levi and Present Priests Contrasted (2:4-9)

a. The Reverence of Levi (2:4-5). Now that the Lord has described the sins of the priests and the curse which they have brought upon themselves, He contrasts the present priests with the faithful priests of the past. First, in verse 4, God explains that "this commandment," the decree of punishment of verses 2-3, was sent so that the Levitical priesthood may continue. Judgment had to fall so that "you will know" that the Lord has spoken. This expression is similar to Ezekiel's frequent line, "Then you will know that I am the Lord," after destruction and devastation have come (Eze 15:7; 33:29).

The covenant was made with Levi in that a member of the tribe of Levi, Aaron, became the first high priest, and his descendants served as priests throughout Israel's history. Hence, in verses 4-9, "Levi" is used in the sense of the Levitical priesthood.

The covenant with Levi is called one of life and peace, in verse 5, for the priests were deeply concerned about the physical and spiritual lives of the people and their well-being before God. As already noted, the famous priestly blessing of Numbers 6:24-26 concludes with the request that the Lord "give you peace." This peace involves more than cessation from war. It contains the ideas of wholeness, soundness, and prosperity, as well as peace with God.

The meaning of "life and peace" in this context is best illustrated from the historical reference in Numbers 25:12, where "My covenant of peace" was first mentioned. The covenant was "given" or confirmed to Phinehas, the grandson of Aaron, who checked a plague against Israel by killing Zimri and the Midianite woman he had brought into the Israelite community. This was one of the saddest episodes in Israel's history, when the people worshiped the Baal of Peor and committed fornication with the Moabite women. At a time when thousands were succumbing to idolatry and sexual immorality, Phinehas, the priest, was jealous on God's behalf and turned away God's wrath from Israel (Num 25:11).

It seems strange to mention a "covenant of peace" in a context so filled with turmoil, but peace with God involves dealing with sin. Isaiah 53:5 describes the punishment that Christ took to procure our "well-being" or "peace." Unfortunately, the priests Malachi addresses were not concerned in the least about their own sinful actions, let alone the sins that were robbing the people of peace with God.

The attitude of Phinehas was one of reverence and respect for God, in contrast to the attitude of the priests in 1:6. This "fear of God," to which Malachi so often refers, was evident in Phinehas' zeal for the Laws of God. He "stood in awe of My name," while the priests of Malachi's day scorned that same name. Actually, the verbs *to revere* and *to stand in awe* in 1:5 occur together frequently in a combination translated, "Do not fear or be dismayed" (Deu 1:21; Jer 1:17). God encourages His servants not to be afraid of man and his power, because God is on their side. In a profound way, they are to "fear and be dismayed" before God.

Isaiah 8:9-13 contains the same view of the awesome God. Since God is holy, He should be the object of Isaiah's "fear" and "dread" (Is 8:13). Significantly, Isaiah 8:9 speaks of the nations being "shattered" before God, and *shattered* is the same word translated "dismayed," or, in Malachi 2:5, "stood in awe." Ours is a majestic and mighty God, before whom we should bow in humble adoration. Yet our tendency is to ignore God and to be afraid of men and of what they will think of us.

b. The Faithful Instruction of Levi (2:6-7). Verses 6-7 go on to describe the faithful priest as a man of integrity, walking in close fellowship with God. "The law of truth" was in his mouth, which could mean either that he was characterized by truthful instruction or that the Mosaic Law was often on his lips. "Law" can also signify "principle," as in Proverbs 31:26, where the ideal wife has "the law of kindness" on her tongue. Every word is to be governed by the principle of kindness or truth.

Since *law* often means the Mosaic Law or the Word of God in general (Torah), certainly *truth* can be applied specifically to "the Law." Psalm 119:142 says that God's Law is truth, and the priests were known as the experts in the Law. Part of their function was to teach the people the statutes of Moses (Lev 10:11) and to "handle the law" (Jer 2:8). When specific verdicts were required in difficult legal cases, the priests sometimes served as judges (Deu 17:9-11; see also the discussion at Hag 2:11).

This dual responsibility to teach and to judge accounts for the emphasis upon truth and honesty in the verse. Unrighteousness or perverting of the truth was not to be found on their lips. The tongue is often implicated in deceitfulness or injustice (Job 13:7; Is 59:3), but godly priests were to walk "in peace and uprightness." Their words and actions were to be "on the level" and above reproach.

"Peace" and "righteousness" are linked in several other passages also, for without justice and purity there can be no real peace. Isaiah 60:17 speaks of a government with peace as administrators and righteousness as overseers. In Psalm 85:10 not only have righteousness and peace "kissed each other," but "truth" is joined with "lovingkindness." The similarities with Malachi 2:6 are obvious. *Truth* is a word often connected with faithfulness to a covenant or agreement. In Joshua 2:14, it is used of adhering "faithfully" to the terms agreed upon by Rahab and the Israelite spies. Since the Levitical covenant is mentioned both in verses 4 and 8, the actions described in verse 6 clearly involve loyalty to that covenant.

The instruction from the Word of God and the example of priests should result in turning many people away from iniquity. This "turning" could refer to repentance through conviction of sin or to preventing individuals from falling into sin. Because of the exalted position of priests as the representatives of God, their influence did indeed affect *many*. Daniel 12:3 describes the blessed status of "those who lead the many to righteousness." Among the leaders of Israel, this privilege and responsibility belonged above all to the priests.

The seventh verse amplifies the mission of the priests, for they were the ones who "preserve knowledge," that is, who treasure the Law and store it in their hearts and minds (1 Ch 29:18). "The fear of the LORD is the beginning of knowledge" (Pr 1:7), a fact which may account for the repetition of the "fear" motif throughout Malachi. Knowledge that starts with respect for the Lord involves a personal relationship with God. Men were to consult the priests not only because they knew the facts about God's Word but because they were vitally in tune with God.

So close was their relationship with God that they could be called "messengers" of the Lord. This is a lofty title also applied to prophets, as in Haggai 1:13. The priests were the "ordinary messengers" of God, while the prophets were the "extraordinary messengers."[6] The term itself can be translated "angel" equally well, for angels are God's supernatural ministers. In Malachi 3:1, "messenger" assumes great importance as it refers to the ministry of John the Baptist and of Christ Himself. To be a "messenger of the Lord" was a high and holy calling. Believers are called "ambassadors for Christ," commissioned to spread the gospel to a world in desperate need (2 Co 5:20).

c. *The Corrupt Instruction of the Priests* (2:8-9). The gap between the ideal and the real is painfully obvious in verses 8-9. Instead of instructing the people in the ways of the Lord, they have deviated from the high standards outlined in verses 6-7. Ironically, the people were warned in Deuteronomy 17:11 not to "turn aside" from the instructions of the priests. But now the priests themselves are guilty of "turning aside." No longer are they turning people from sin; rather, they cause many to stumble by their wicked behavior and false teaching. The priests are placing stumbling blocks in the path of the people to bring about the downfall of the whole nation.

In summary, God accuses the priests of corrupting the covenant of Levi. They are ruining the priesthood and stifling the spiritual growth of the tiny country. Nehemiah describes contemporary priests as those who defiled the priesthood and the Levitical covenant by contracting marriages with foreigners (Neh 13:27). Malachi faces this problem head-on in verses 10-16.

Another example of priestly corruption concerns their tendency to show partiality "in the instruction" (v. 9). Being partial is literally "lifting up the face" or "showing favor" (see comments on 1:8-9), but it sometimes connotes giving special favors because of bribes (Pr 6:35). Judges were ordered not to show partiality to either rich or poor (Lev 19:15) but to be fair in their decisions. Since priests often had judicial functions (Deu 17:9-11), 2:9 probably refers to their role as administrators of justice. God Himself is impartial and incapable of being bribed

6. C. F. Keil, *The Twelve Minor Prophets*, 2:446.

(Deu 10:17), and the priests as His representatives should be equally honest in rendering decisions.

In light of the priests' perversion of justice and overall negligence, God had to make them "despised and abased before all the people." Their actions brought on a humiliation not at all in keeping with their high office, but one they fully deserved. The same priests who despised the name of the Lord in 1:6 and who considered the sacrificial system despicable in 1:7 and 12 are now themselves held in contempt. Psalm 15:4 says that a reprobate ought to be despised, but those who fear the Lord should be honored. Sadly, the priests clearly belonged in the former category.

9

The Failures of the People

III. THE UNFAITHFULNESS OF THE PEOPLE (2:10-16)

A. The People Have Broken Their Covenant with God (2:10-12)

JUST AS A CHURCH is not likely to rise above the spiritual level of its pastor, so the people of Israel faltered along with the priests. The nation grew cold toward their God and began to find foreign idols more attractive. This led to serious problems in the home also, as divorce became common, and corruption permeated all areas of life.

1. *The Worship of Foreign Gods* (2:10-11)

Verses 10-16 in many ways reflect the evils that plagued the priesthood, but the mention of Judah, Israel, and Jacob broadens the perspective to include the entire nation. The priests are perhaps more guilty of these sins than the people at large, and, in fact, they have led the people into wickedness. Yet, the nation as a whole is responsible for their actions and must bear the blame along with the priests.

Malachi switches to the first person plural in verse 10, an indication that God is no longer being quoted. The prophet identifies himself with the people as he wonders why they are behaving like this and asks, "Do we not all have one father?" This could be taken to refer to their racial unity as descendants of Abraham, but the parallelism with "one God" argues against this, along with the designation of God as Father of the nation in 1:6. In Isaiah 63:16, God is identified as more of a Father to Israel than either Abraham or Jacob. Agreeing with this are the Jews of Jesus' day, who claim, "We have one Father, even God" (Jn 8:41).

The Fatherhood of God is generally restricted in the Old Testament to the relationship between God and Israel. There is no justification for applying the brotherhood of man to the whole world, for in verse 11, God condemns marriage with foreigners who worship other gods. Their "fathers" cannot be equated with the Father of Israel. Even the reference to God as Creator can point to His work in forming Israel as His own special nation. The people God has called by name are created as His possession to proclaim His praise (Ex 19:5; Is 43:1, 7, 21). Malachi 3:17 also speaks of God's "special treasure," or, "possession," reflecting the language of Exodus 19:5, when God singled out Israel.

Although they were uniquely related to God, Israel seemed intent upon destroying this relationship; and Malachi wonders why. The people are dealing treacherously with one another, thus violating the covenant with God. Their treachery is the main theme of verses 10-16, being mentioned five times within that span. Some interpreters hold that this treachery consists of marrying foreign women in 10-12 and of divorcing their Israelite wives in 14-16. While it is true that the people were guilty of both sins, it appears that the primary charge of verses 10-12 is "marriage" with foreign gods.

"Treachery" is mainly applied in Scripture to the breaking of a covenant, usually the marriage covenant. Since the husband-wife relationship is used often of God and Israel, "marriage" terminology is as suitable as the parent-child analogy. "As a woman treacherously departs from her lover, So you have dealt treacherously with Me, O house of Israel" (Jer 3:20). The nation, like their forefathers, betrayed God by breaking the covenant (Ps 78:57). They were as unfaithful and unreliable as a "wadi," a stream that runs dry during summer heat (Job 6:15).

"The covenant of our fathers" is broader than the "Levitical covenant" of verses 5 and 8, referring rather to the covenant made at Mt. Sinai with the entire nation. At that time God became a husband to the nation (Jer 31:32), and unlike Israel, He did not violate the agreement made (Ps 89:35).

The people were dealing treacherously "each against his brother," which implies more than marriage irregularities. One could not trust the members of his own family! Relatives and neighbors were liable to betray each other (Jer 9:4; 12:6). It probably also refers to the favoritism of verse 9 and the general corruption of Judean leaders. Zephaniah 3:4 is remarkably similar to Malachi, as it describes life in Judah not long before the fall of Jerusalem:

> Her prophets are reckless, treacherous men;
> Her priests have profaned the sanctuary.
> They have done violence to the law.

Each of these indictments applied to Malachi's day, and verse 11 includes the identical expression "Judah [and especially the priests!] has profaned the sanctuary." Chapter one has already explained partially how they polluted it.

In a sense, the sanctuary of the Lord is the nation itself (Ps 114:2). They were set apart to be a holy people but were now acting like a pagan nation. Their sin is called "an abomination," a term reserved for the worst of evils, such as immorality, witchcraft, or idolatry. The mention of "a foreign god" specifies "idolatry" as the sin in question. Judah "has married the daughter of a foreign god." The word *married* is the root of the noun *baal*, meaning "lord, master, husband." Best known as the name of the Canaanite god "Baal," the verb was likely chosen to allude again to Numbers 25:3, where Israel "joined up" with the Baal of Peor and incurred God's anger. The Lord demands the exclusive worship of His people.

One way to become involved with foreign gods is to marry foreign women, a practice forbidden in Exodus 34:11-16. The relationship with Moabite girls paved the way to idolatry in Numbers 25, and Solomon succumbed in similar fashion. Nehemiah, in fact, referred to Solomon as he condemned intermarriage with women from Ashdod, Ammon, and Moab (Neh 13:23-29). A few decades earlier, Ezra had wrestled with the same problem, discovering that many Jews had taken Canaanite wives after returning from Babylon (Ezra 9:1-3). It is only a matter of time before pagan women lead their husbands into sin and the worship of other gods. With good reason, Paul asks, "What has a believer in common with an unbeliever?" (2 Co 6:15). The apostle then adds in the very next verse, "Or what agreement has the temple of God with idols?" The personal "temple" should not be polluted any more than the sanctuary standing in Jerusalem.

2. *The Response of God* (2:12)

A man who violates the covenant of the Lord and enters any kind of relationship with a foreign god is subject to strong condemnation. Such a person will find that his family will eventually be wiped out, for the Lord will "cut off . . . everyone who awakes and answers." Whatever the exact meaning of the obscure "awakes and answers," it must refer to a man's posterity. Some interpret it to mean "teacher and student" or "watcher and respondent." The latter combination is a distinct possibility, since "watcher" finds support from Daniel 4:13 and 17. Yet the idea of cutting off a watchman and respondents sounds more like destroying a whole city than a single family.

"Awakes and answers" has the added advantage of reproducing the alliteration found in the Hebrew. Perhaps "who awakes" could be better handled "who is awake" in the sense of "alive." Daniel 12:2 refers to the dead as those "who sleep in the dust." One who is "awake" is thus a living person who is able to answer, to respond, and show signs of life. The English expression of being "alive and kicking" may not be far from the thrust of this Hebrew idiom.

Also to be cut off is one who could present an offering to the Lord. The guilty individual will have no survivor in his family to worship the Lord by participating in the sacrificial system. Actually the description would best fit a priestly family, because they were the ones who normally presented the offerings to the Lord. In Malachi itself, the role of the priests in presenting offerings is mentioned twice (1:7 and 3:3), so the prophet may be pointing his finger at the Levitical family in particular. The language is reminiscent of the judgment that struck Eli, whose family was cut off from the priesthood because of his negligence and the wickedness of his two sons (1 Sa 2:29-35).

The descendants of the guilty man are to be cut off "from the tents of Jacob," an expression that looks back to the humble beginning of the nation but also to their privileged position as the people of God. They consisted of one large family gathered around the sanctuary of God. In Jeremiah 30:18, "tents" is a poetic parallel for "dwelling places."

B. The People Have Broken Their Marriage Vows (2:13-16)

1. God Refuses to Accept Their Offerings (2:13)

One "abomination" has outraged God in verses 11-12, and now Malachi turns to a second closely related aspect of their unfaithfulness, the abomination of divorce. Before pinpointing the sin itself, the prophet discusses some of the consequences of that sin: God seems distant and is no longer accepting their offerings. In chapter one, the Lord refused to accept any of their sacrifices because the animals were sadly defective (1:8, 10, 13), but here a different reason for divine displeasure is introduced.

The people were intent on having the Lord regard the offering, that is, receive it with favor (Num 16:15), for they were almost drenching the altar "with tears, with weeping and with groaning." This is a description of earnest prayer, begging God to take action and even to save one's life (Ps 39:12; Is 38:3). Tears and groaning are also characteristic of lamenting or mourning the death of loved ones (1 Sa 2:33; Eze 24:16-17).

Here, in verse 13, the people are complaining that God is not paying any attention to them, much like the hypocrites Isaiah mentioned, who fasted and became irritable and oppressive—and then wondered why God did not acknowledge their spirituality! (Is 58:2-6).

Some interpreters feel that the tearful ones were the divorced women, who were driven to prayer by the unfairness of their former husbands. Nothing in the text leads to such a conclusion, however, since weeping and groaning are as much masculine traits in the biblical world as they are feminine. All of the references in the previous paragraph deal with the weeping of men.

2. *Divorce Is the Reason for God's Displeasure* (2:14)

For the first time since 1:13, "Yet you say" occurs as the people ask, "Why, Lord? Why don't you respond?" The answer is a direct one, because the people are guilty of betraying the bond of trust into which they had entered at marriage. As in verse 10, "treachery" is used to describe the action.

By marrying the daughter of a foreign god, an Israelite spurned the true God, and he was also rejecting his first wife, resulting in a divorce. Yet this goes against the sacred nature and the true meaning of marriage. God was a witness when the two partners pledged their loyalty to one another. Although the Bible says little about the place of witnesses at a wedding, marriage documents from Jewish sources do include a list of witnesses. Part of their function was to certify that the bride-price had been paid. A biblical example of witnesses at a marriage may be seen in Isaiah 8:1-3, if my interpretation of that passage is correct.[7] Uriah the priest could have filled our role of "minister" most acceptably.

Witnesses are often involved in making a covenant (Jos 24:

---

7. See *Journal of Biblical Literature*, 91 (1972): 450-53 for a discussion of "witnesses" in the Old Testament and in the Elephantine Jewish papyruses.

22), and significantly, Malachi 2:14 speaks of "your wife by covenant." Marriage is indeed a covenant, as shown also in Proverbs 2:17 and Ezekiel 16:8. The Proverbs passage condemns a woman "that leaves the companion of her youth, and forgets the covenant of her God." The parallel would indicate that this woman is violating the marriage agreement made before God with her husband. In Malachi the reverse is true, with the husband being the guilty party.

Proverbs' expression "the companion of her youth" matches Malachi's "the wife of your youth." It is the partner one chose in the full flush of youthful love. As young people, they fell deeply in love and reveled in each other's companionship. But over the years, instead of deepening and growing, their love had become cold, and particularly the husband was tempted to trade in his wife for a younger woman. Perhaps the foreign women were more beautiful, enticing him to break the marriage bond. Proverbs 5:18 exhorts husbands to "rejoice in the wife of your youth" and not to seek a thrill from some other woman.

According to God's original design, marriage was a permanent relationship, and a man was instructed to leave his parents and cling to his wife. In the words of Genesis 2:24, "They shall become one flesh." Something of this unity is seen in the word *companion,* which means "joined together, united." A striking illustration of this oneness is seen in Judges 20:11, where the men of Israel gathered to fight a wicked city and they pressed on "united as one man." The word *united* is the same as Malachi's "companion." It implies harmony, a desire to work together to achieve life's greatest goals while sharing all the hardship, the pain, and the joy. In every sense of the word, husband and wife should be inseparable (Mt 19:6).

3. *God's Sharp Rebuke* (2:15-16)

Having given the reason for His anger with the people, God further denounces their actions in verses 15-16. Verse 16 is directly quoting the Lord, and verse 15 may be part of that quotation. Essentially the fifteenth verse refutes the argument that, since Abraham married a foreigner and obtained a divorce, both practices are permissible for his descendants. The verse is written in compact and concise Hebrew, and the difficulties are reflected in the variety of translations. From my perspective, the text of the New American Standard Bible is the most accurate here, if the reader distinguishes between "not one" and "that one." "Not one," that is, "nobody" who has any spiritual insight has ever betrayed his wife. The Spirit of God would never lead anyone to take such drastic action. Some commentators interpret "spirit" as "sense" or "reasoning power." Then the verse would mean that no one who has an "ounce of sense" would ever behave like this.

After the opening clause, the verse inserts a few words which could be translated, "And what about the one?" or, "And what did the one do?" "The one" must refer to the father of the Jewish people, the renowned giant of the faith, Abraham (Is 51:2). Was he not a spiritual man, and did he not marry an Egyptian, Hagar, and then proceed to divorce her? The incident was well known to every Jew, so Malachi is able to deal with this objection very quickly.

Yes, Abraham did marry a foreigner, but, "he was seeking a godly offspring," and the situation was entirely different. Abraham married Hagar at the suggestion of his wife, Sarah, in accordance with a custom known from Mesopotamia (Gen 16:1-3). God had promised an heir, but since Sarah was barren, she suggested that her servant become Abraham's wife and produce the heir for her. Both Sarah and Abraham were concerned about the son God had promised, and they were "helping" God by involving Hagar. Unlike the Jews of Malachi's time, Abraham was not overcome with carnal passion when he took Hagar. His motivation was good, although he was wrong in marrying Hagar, and the children of Ishmael and Isaac have been fighting ever since.

The appeal to Abraham's divorce was even more fallacious.

Abraham had no desire to divorce Hagar, and he sent her away only after God specifically told him to do so (Gen 21:10). Besides, Sarah was "the wife of his youth," and Abraham remained faithful to her. It was the foreign wife who was divorced.

Therefore, "Take heed to your spirit" and do not betray your Israelite wives. For the second time in the verse, "spirit" is ambiguous. The whole idiom is close to "watch yourselves carefully"; yet the warning deals with their spiritual lives, so the English equivalent falls somewhat short. Moses told Israel to "watch their souls" lest they become involved with idolatry (Deu 4:15), and Joshua used the same idiom to promote love for God and to discourage intermarriage with pagan nations (Jos 23:11-12). Both passages have close affinities with the context of Malachi 2.

In God's infallible opinion, divorce is a terrible thing, deserving of His hatred. These strong words at the start of verse 16 underscore the divine viewpoint on the permanence of marriage. Yes, Moses did make provision for husbands to divorce their wives (Deu 24:1-3), but Christ attributed this to the hardness of man's hearts and not to divine design (Mt 19:7-8). There were no "easy" divorces and casual switching of partners under Moses' Law—unlike modern society. If the wife was not guilty of immorality, she could not be divorced, so the man Malachi addresses had no grounds for divorce.

Several times in Scripture, divorce became necessary because of the wickedness of the wives. Twice, God speaks of giving Israel a "certificate of divorce," owing to her immoral idolatry, her religious "prostitution" (Is 50:1; Jer 3:8) with foreign princes and gods! The Lord had to send her out of the land, for the relationship was badly broken. In the nation's history, this period of separation or divorce corresponds to the seventy years of exile.[8]

8. Hosea may also have divorced his wife temporarily because of her adulterous behavior (Ho 2:2 and 3:1-3), thus empathizing with God's agony over Israel.

Another instance of divorce occurred in Ezra 10:3, 19, a situation very similar to the one faced by Malachi. The returned exiles had intermarried, and Ezra's preaching brought them under conviction. As a result, they covenanted "to put away" their wives and send them back to their native lands. The term *put away* (lit., "cause to go out") is not used of divorce elsewhere, however, and it may indicate the illegality of the marriages in the first place (Cp. Ezra 9:1 and Ex 34:11-16). Intermarriage was even more serious back in 460 BC, since the small Jewish remnant Ezra confronted was in danger of being wholly absorbed by the surrounding nations.

A second object of God's hatred is the "one who covers his garment with wrong" or, literally, with "violence." This is a person who clothes himself with violence, even as the psalmist describes the man who "clothed himself with cursing as with his garment" (Ps 109:18). It is worn where all can see it, reflecting the inward condition of such a man. When hearts are brought to repentance, men cover themselves with sackcloth (Jon 3:6), but the proud adorn themselves with violence (Ps 73:6).

Violence is a strong term, sometimes even linked with murder (Hab 2:8). The priests were charged by Zephaniah with doing violence to the Law (Zep 3:4), which could correspond to the sin of playing fast and loose with divorce contrary to the Law. Yet, to restrict "violence" to divorce in Malachi may be overstating the case. The treachery of 2:10 apparently includes corruption in court and in religious life. And when Malachi closes verse 16 by repeating the warning of verse 15, "Take heed . . . that you do not deal treacherously," he omits the words, *against the wife of your youth*. Undoubtedly, this phrase is implied in verse 16, but "treachery" also has the broader meaning first seen in verse 10.

10

The Approaching Judgment

IV. THE COMING OF GOD'S MESSENGER IN JUDGMENT (2:17—4:6)

A. The Coming of the Messenger of the Covenant to Purify and Punish (2:17—3:6)

THE SERIOUS NATURE of the sin of the priests and the people at large inevitably brings God's judgment. Rather than sending an angel or a plague, God will personally intervene both to purify and to punish the stubborn nation. The judging aspects of His coming were intended to challenge the people to forsake their sinful practices and to serve the Lord faithfully. There was still time to repent.

1. *The Question About God's Justice* (2:17)

In the first two chapters, Malachi has given the reader clear insight into the disgraceful attitudes and actions of the priests and the people. Now, in 2:17 the prophet explains part of the motivation behind such sinful behavior. The people did not think that God cared whether they were good or bad, since He did not seem to punish the wicked or reward the righteous. Verses 13-15 of chapter 3 elaborate on the latter complaint. Perhaps 2:17 is a reaction to the Lord's denouncement of divorce and violence. If the Persians and other pagan peoples get away with terrible crimes, and if the wicked within Israel tend to prosper the most, is God really actively involved in the affairs of men? Is He not "showing partiality" as a judge (2:9)?

According to Malachi, these complaints have wearied the Lord. In 1:13 the priests were tired of the whole sacrificial system, and now they have succeeded in exhausting God. How can mere man exhaust "the everlasting God," who "does not become weary or tired"? (Is 40:28). Isaiah himself best explains the anthropomorphism: Israel had wearied God with their sin (Is 1:14; 43:24), and Ahaz had exhausted the patience of God by refusing to ask for a sign in his persistent unbelief (Is 7:11-13).

The specific charge against the Lord, in verse 17, is that "everyone who does evil is good" in His sight. Nothing could be further from the truth, because God consistently pronounced "woe to those who call evil good, and good evil" (Is 5:20). Justifying the wicked is "an abomination to the Lord" (Pr 17:15), the same strong word employed in Malachi 2:11. God does not delight in the wicked any more than He delighted in those who offered defective sacrifices (1:10). As the psalmist puts it, God is not One "who takes pleasure in wickedness" (5:4). He delights in justice, lovingkindness, and humility (Mic 6:8).

The people, however, are skeptical, so they ask, "Where is the God of justice?" Why does He not do something to demonstrate His power and justice? Others had voiced the same sentiments to earlier prophets. Isaiah's "Holy One of Israel" was urged to take swift action to prove His ability (Is 5:19), and Jeremiah was taunted to produce evidence that the Lord's predictions would come to pass (Jer 17:15). Yet, by asking for God to reveal His justice, the sinners in Judah were bringing on themselves the judgment of that God. The same Hebrew word can be translated either "justice" or "judgment" (3:5).

2. *The Sudden Coming of the Lord to His Temple* (3:1)

Chapter three should have begun with 2:17, because 3:1 is a direct reply to the question posed in the preceding verse. It almost appears as if Malachi were eagerly anticipating their question, because the answer given is full and powerful. Indeed, this is a famous and crucial verse, focusing on the coming messengers of the Lord, and "My messenger" is in Hebrew "malachi," the same as the author's name (see Introduction).

With little hesitation one can identify "My messenger" with John the Baptist. This verse is quoted in Matthew 11:10, Mark 1:2, and Luke 1:76, referring to John's work of preparing the way of the Lord. In addition, Malachi 4:5 mentions the coming of Elijah, and Elijah is also identified with John the Baptist in the New Testament (Mt 11:14; Lk 1:17). A messenger is normally a prophet, and none appeared from the time of Malachi until John arrived on the scene some 450 years later, preaching in the tradition of Malachi.

The task of the messenger is to "clear the way before Me," an expression citing Isaiah 40:3, 57:14, and 62:10. "To clear the way" means to remove the stones from the road (Is 62:10), to get rid of every obstacle or stumbling block that might be in the way (Is 57:14). In Malachi 2:8, the Lord condemned the priests who were causing the people to stumble by their teaching. This made necessary the work of the messenger in removing those obstacles as he led the people to repent of their injustice and unbelief.

Scripture also uses this idiom of "clearing the ground" so that a vine, representing Israel, can be planted and take deep root (Ps 80:9; cf. Mt 3:10). Then in Genesis 24:31, it means to "clean up" a house for the visiting servant of Abraham (cf. Mt 3:12). The preaching of John the Baptist was aimed at a massive housecleaning within the nation of Israel, the "house of Jacob." Spiritually they were in no condition to welcome the heavenly Visitor. Tragically, many people will be equally unprepared to meet the Lord when He returns a second time.

God declares that John will prepare the way "before Me," and, in the next sentence, identifies "Me" with "the Lord" and "the messenger of the covenant." Plainly, the incarnation of the second Person of the Trinity is intended, although the One who sends "My messenger" is perhaps the Father. "The Lord" is the sovereign One, the Almighty God, whose authority is supreme. This particular word for "Lord" occurs as "master" in 1:6 and as the One whose table is being polluted in 1:12.

Since the sovereign One is coming to His Temple, those who polluted that sanctuary are due to be judged. The priests, who considered ministering there as something despicable (1:7, 10, 12), could hardly look forward to the coming of "the Master." When, in fact, Christ visited the Temple, He did drive out the money-changers and all who were misusing the sanctuary (Jn 2:14-15). The majesty of the coming Lord may be reflected in the word for "Temple." It can also mean "palace," for it is a structure suitable for a king. Twice this word is used for "temple" in Haggai (Hag 2:15, 18), and the same building is in view here, namely Zerubbabel's Temple modified by Herod.

The Lord's coming will be a sudden one, when people least expect it, but when God's timing is right. For Herod the Great, the search of the wise men for another king of the Jews took him by surprise and deeply disturbed him (Mt 2:3). Even John the Baptist needed divine help in recognizing the Lamb of God (Jn 1:31-34).

Another title for the Lord is "the messenger of the covenant," who must be distinguished from "My messenger" earlier in the verse. The parallelism clearly links this "messenger" with the Lord. In this case the double meaning of "messenger-angel" also aids the interpretation, for the "angel of the covenant" reminds one of the "Angel of the Lord," a divine title. "Covenant" may be utilized to recall the Levitical covenant (2:4, 8) and the Sinaitic or Mosaic covenant (2:10), which figure prominently in Malachi. The priestly "messengers" (2:7) failed to keep either covenant, but this new "messenger" will establish a new covenant and a new priesthood (Heb 8:8-13). As the Angel of the Lord in the Old Testament economy, He was intimately connected with the making of the Mosaic covenant (Judg 2:1-2). It was this Angel who led Israel out of Egypt (Ex 14:19) and brought them into the promised land (Ex 23:20).

Since the Angel of the Lord did not pardon transgressions (Ex

23:21), it is hard to understand why, in 3:1, the sinful Jews were seeking Him and delighting in Him. Does this mean they were seeking Him only in the context of the question, "Where is the God of justice?" (2:17), or were some of the people genuinely looking for His coming? The Messianic hope persisted throughout Israel's history, even in the postexilic period (Dan 9:25; Hag 2:7, 23). Another alternative is to take "seek" and "delight" in a sarcastic sense. They professed to be seeking the Lord, but in reality, they were only going through the motions (Is 58:2) while Malachi was exposing their true attitudes.

One fact was certain: He was coming, and this is underscored by the second use of "behold" in the verse. Doubters in the past kept asking for God's word to come to pass (Jer 17:15); God now promised that His messenger, the Word of God incarnate, would come on the scene.

3. The Purifying Work of the Lord (3:2-4)

a. The Power of His Coming (3:2). Even if the people were sincerely seeking the coming of the Lord, one can be sure that they had a wrong concept of His mission. They hoped that He would destroy the Gentile powers and restore the power of Israel, but they were not prepared for His work of purifying the Jews. After all, "Who can endure the day of His coming?" Known as "the Day of the Lord," this would be an awesome period (Joel 2:11), in which none of the nations could hold their own. "At His wrath the earth quakes," and no country can withstand His indignation (Jer 10:10). The Lord is a consuming fire (Deu 4:24), and on the great day of His wrath, "Who is able to stand?" (Rev 6:16-17). Malachi 4:1-3 further discusses the nature of the coming day.

Obviously, most of the passages just cited deal with the second coming of Christ, when the judging work of the Lord will be climaxed. Malachi presents a blend of the first and second comings of Christ, as is the case in the closely parallel Isaiah 40:1-11, and also in Isaiah 61:1-2. Even the first coming of

Christ was not without its judgmental side, however, particularly against the scribes and Pharisees (Jn 9:39). The cleansing of the Temple also revealed the anger of the Lord (Jn 2:13-17), the One John the Baptist said would baptize with the Holy Spirit and with fire (Is 4:4; Mt 3:11).

According to Psalm 24:3-4, the person who may stand in God's holy place must have "clean hands and a pure heart." But man is sinful and can claim no intrinsic cleanness (Ps 130:3; Is 6:5). Surely the Jewish people, living in the sin portrayed in Malachi 1-2, will not be able to stand before the all-powerful Messenger. All are in need of the refining, cleansing work of God.

The refining process purifies a metal from all its alloys and dross. Applying the heat burns out whatever is worthless, leaving a pure product. The metaphor is sometimes used of purging a person from sin, for God is the One who tests us and refines us like silver (Ps 66:10). At times, the refining seems to be ineffective (Jer 6:29-30), but the fires of judgment will eventually purify the remnant as silver and gold are refined (Zec 13:9).

Malachi connects the "refiner's fire" with "fuller's soap," referring to a second cleansing process. The "fuller" was the laundryman, who cleaned clothes by trampling on them until the dirt was removed. A strong soap was used in this process, a kind of lye or bleach. Shining white clothes were a symbol of purity (Rev 3:5), and on the mount of transfiguration, Christ's garments were whiter than any "launderer on earth can whiten them" (Mk 9:3).

Israel had tried to wash itself with lye, but the stain of sin remained (Jer 2:22; 4:14). In view of the garment covered with violence, mentioned in Malachi 2:16, additional cleansing action was badly needed. Many had to be "purged, purified" (lit., "made white") and "refined" (Dan 12:10). Isaiah 1:25, like Daniel, combines the figures of refining and washing as the Lord promises He "will smelt away your dross as with lye," in order to produce a righteous city. Both processes are radical ones, signifying the hand of God in judgment.

b. The Purifying of the Priests and Their Offerings (3:3-4). Since so much emphasis has been placed upon the pitiful condition of the priests, and since the priests as ministers of God should have been examples of purity, the Lord describes their judgment first. They are called "the sons of Levi," but the priestly branch of Levi, the descendants of Aaron, are clearly intended (cf. 1:6; 2:1, 4).

The Lord will sit as a smelter (or refiner) and purifier of silver to cleanse the priests. "Sitting" may designate God's position as King, seated on a throne to rule and judge. This is the only instance in the Old Testament where this particular word, *to purify,* is used of metal. Normally, it has reference to matters of ritual cleanness, such as the purification of the Temple (2 Ch 29:15-16), or of the priests (Neh 13:30). An offering can also be called "pure" (Mal 1:11). The reference in Nehemiah 13 declares that the governor purified the priests "from everything foreign," including some foreign wives. How suitable to the context of Malachi (2:10-12)!

A different word for "refine" is inserted in the middle of verse 3, a term connoting the "straining" or "filtering" used in the refining process (Is 25:6). In 1 Chronicles, the word appears twice to describe the "refined gold" used for the altar of incense and the "refined silver" to adorn the walls of the Temple (1 Ch 28:18; 29:4). If the sanctuary was "refined," the ministers who served there should have been equally pure. Based on Isaiah 1:25-28, this "refining" involved the destruction of the rebellious and the restoration of those who repented.

The presentation of acceptable offerings was the object of this purification. Offerings would be brought "in righteousness." Does this refer to the spiritual condition of the priest or to the "unblemished" condition of the sacrificial animal? Both were woefully defective, according to chapter 1, and both are needed for a proper offering. Psalm 4:5 emphasizes the heart attitude of the offerer, while Psalm 51:19 stresses the condition of the animal. After a sinner has truly repented, *then* God will "delight in righteous sacrifices."

Malachi 3:4, like Psalm 51:19, records the Lord's acceptance of the right kind of offering. When a priest who is walking in fellowship with God (2:6) presents a healthy animal or a proper grain offering, it will be pleasing to the Lord. The term *be pleasing* is a synonym for "be acceptable, received with favor," found in 1:10, 13, and 2:13 (cf. Jer 6:20). Such an offering would be as pleasant and as refreshing as sleep (Jer 31:26) to God, who had been "wearied" by their wickedness (2:17).

This is the only time in Malachi that "Judah and Jerusalem" are mentioned together (although 2:11 comes close). Prominent as a combination in Isaiah (1:1; 2:1), their occurrence may be another indication that Malachi was drawing upon the earlier prophet. The first verses of chapter 3 have many ties with the great writing of Isaiah.

The restoration of the sacrificial system will resemble conditions "in the days of old." Some equate these "former years" with the days of Moses and the early priests (2:4-5). Others point to the golden years of the United Kingdom, when David strengthened the worship of Israel and Solomon built the Temple. Perhaps the reference to Phinehas in Malachi 2 tips the scales in favor of the Mosaic period.

More difficult to determine are the nature and time of the fulfillment of this prophecy. Is Malachi talking about literal sacrifices or about the "sacrifice of praise" (Heb 13:15) and the "living sacrifice" of the New Testament? (Ro 12:1). Many priests became believers in Christ (Ac 6:7), and Barnabas was an outstanding Levite (Ac 4:36). Many of the issues involved have already been analyzed in the comments regarding 1:11. Those who favor a literal fulfillment cite such passages as Ezekiel 44:15 or Zechariah 14:21, which refer to the offering of sacrifices during the millennial period. Since Christ's second coming is part of the context in Malachi 3, this view has real merit. Isaiah also speaks of restoring judges "as at the first" and counselors "as at the beginning," so that Jerusalem can again become "the city of righteousness" (Is 1:26). Ultimately, this will find fulfillment during the Kingdom age (Is 60:14).

4. *The Punishing Work of the Lord* (3:5)

Using the first person pronoun, as He did in verse 1, the Lord specifies His coming for judgment. This is a direct reply to the question rather flippantly posed in 2:17: "Where is the God of justice [or judgment]?" Verses 2-4 actually deal with the same judging work under the more positive figures of refining and purifying. It is doubtful, therefore, whether verse 5 takes place after verses 2-4. The proper relationship between the verses would probably best be indicated by, "So I will draw near," instead of, "Then." Whereas verses 2-4 stressed the judgment in store for the priests, verse 5 widens the scope to include the entire nation. The same sequence was followed in chapter 2, with the transition coming in verse 10.

The three legal terms in verse 5 introduce the Lord's case against Israel (cf. Ho 4:1-2). *Draw near, judgment,* and *witness* are all words found in the courtroom, and the Lord has abundant evidence to convict the people. Sin after sin is named by the One who is a "swift witness" against His people. The quickness of His testimony corresponds to the suddenness with which He will come to His Temple, in verse 1. The Lord may delay His coming for many years, but when He takes action, it will be swift and decisive.

The sins listed had been persistent problems throughout Israel's history. Beginning with Moses, the prophets had warned the nation about these evils. Sorcerers and their witchcraft were widespread in the Near East, including Canaan (Ex 7:11; Deu 18:10), and they continued to ply their trade on into New Testament days (Ac 8:9).

Adultery was, of course, forbidden in the Ten Commandments (Ex 20:14), but as evident in the divorce problems in Malachi, it had not yet died out. Similarly, swearing falsely, or lying under oath, was denounced by Moses (Lev 19:12) but continued to be practiced by the nation (Jer 5:2; 7:9).

Oppression of the poor and needy was regarded as a heinous sin, and the prophets preached mightily against this injustice. Refusing to pay laborers promptly was condemned in the Mosaic Law (Lev 19:13, Deu 24:14-15) and even in James 5:4. Frequently the rich and powerful were enjoined not to oppress the widow, orphan, and the alien (Deu 24:19-32; Zec 7:10). These three classes are often linked in Scripture, since their rights were easily violated. "Orphan" can also be correctly translated "fatherless" (Eze 22:7). To "turn aside" or "thrust aside" the alien, was to defraud him in court (see comments on 2:9 also). Warnings against depriving the poor and needy of justice are also given in Isaiah 10:2; 29:21 and Amos 5:12.

In summary, individuals guilty of these sins "do not fear" the Lord. By repeating this key phrase, the Lord shows that all sin stems from a lack of respect or reverence for Himself.

5. *The Reason for His Work* (3:6)

God must refine and judge the nation because of who He is, the One who demands holiness. He has promised that the nation will continue as long as day and night continue; He will have mercy on the people of Israel. Yet He must purge out the sinners, for, "Those who forsake the LORD shall come to an end" (Is 1:28). Israel will undergo punishment, but God assures them, "I will not destroy you completely" (Jer 30:11).

Part of the promise hinges on the fact that the Lord does not change. In the words of the Psalmist, "Thou art the same, And Thy years will not come to an end" (102:27). God's Word is equally unchangeable: "My covenant I will not violate, Nor will I alter the utterance of My lips" (Ps 89:34). This parallel passage is especially significant for two reasons. First, the word *alter* can be rendered "change." It is the same word found in Malachi 3:6. Second, the promise not to "violate" the covenant contrasts

sharply with the nation's "profaning" the ancient covenant (Mal
2:10). Again, the identical Hebrew word is involved. God's
faithfulness to the covenant guarantees the continuation of the
nation.

The people are called "sons of Jacob" in verse 6, perhaps
drawing attention to the deceit and treachery that once characterized their father Jacob, "the supplanter" (Gen 27:35-36). Malachi 2:10-16 has shown that deeds of treachery continue to
plague the life of the nation. The use of "sons of Jacob" also
indicates that the "sons of Levi" (3:3) are no longer being addressed exclusively.

B. The Challenge to Purify Their Giving (3:7-12)

1. *The Failure to Bring Tithes and Offerings* (3:7-8)

True to His merciful character, the Lord extends an invitation
to the sinful nation to turn back to God. Unfortunately, the sons
of Jacob had not changed much for centuries, because they
"turned aside" from God's statutes just after they had been issued
on Mt. Sinai (Ex 32:8), and they persisted in their rebellious
attitude. In this respect, the people are following the priests, who
also "have turned aside from the way" (2:8).

Isaiah had earlier expressed a similar plea to the nation: "Return to Him from whom you have deeply defected, O sons of
Israel" (Is 31:6). Closer to Malachi are the words of another
postexilic prophet, Zechariah: "Return to Me . . . that I may
return to you." To "return" meant to "repent," to change one's
course, and head in the opposite direction. God Himself enabled
one to return or repent (Jer 31:18-19), provided that there was
a willingness to be turned. If the nation turned to God in repentance, He would turn to them with the blessings described in
3:10-12.

It was a gracious invitation, because the nation deserved to be
consumed, not consoled. Yet, as oblivious to reality as they
were in 1:6 and 2:17, the people could not understand why they

should return. In what way is it necessary? Have we done anything wrong? Their response almost implies a willingness to correct the mistake. Even more it reflects spiritual density for people to be so far away from God and not to realize it.

A major area in which some heart-searching needed to be done was in giving to the work of God. So the Lord counters their question with one of His own: "Will a man rob God? Yet you are robbing Me!" (v. 8). It is an incredible question, for how can a mere man rob Almighty God? Impossible, but it was happening. In chapter 1, the Lord had condemned the offering of sacrifices that had been stolen (1:13), and, in 3:5, had accused those who oppressed the poor and helpless in society, gaining financial advantage at their expense. These were also forms of stealing from God, but more directly, the people were withholding tithes and contributions. This should have been obvious to them, but in their obstinacy they played ignorant: "How have we robbed Thee?"

Tithes and contributions had been instituted in the time of Moses and were often a barometer of the nation's spiritual condition. They belonged to the Lord along with burnt offerings, sacrifices, votive offerings, and the firstborn of the flocks and herds (Deu 12:6). The tithe was a tenth of all one's income, the produce from the fields and fruit trees (Lev 27:30; Deu 14:22). Since the Levites had no land of their own, the tithe belonged to them (Num 18:21). Normally the tithe was brought to the sanctuary in Jerusalem and used in a sacrificial meal (Deu 14:22-27). Every third year, however, the tithe was to be used in one's own town for the Levites, aliens, orphans, and widows (Deu 14:29). Failure to tithe was thus another way to oppress the poor (3:5).

The "contributions" or "heave-offerings" are closely related to the tithe. In fact, the Levites, who received the tithe, were required to give a "tithe of the tithe" to the priests as a "contribution" (Num 18:26-29). Whenever a census was taken, each person had to contribute half a shekel to the Lord (Ex 30:13-

15). Sometimes the contributions were purely voluntary. "Every man whose heart moves him" was to contribute money and materials for the building of the tabernacle (Ex 25:2-3; 35:5), and a similar offering was taken by Ezra for the house of God (Ezra 8:25).

During the reign of Hezekiah, a great revival broke out, and one of the results was the faithful giving of tithes and offerings (2 Ch 31:5, 12, 19). After the exile, there were periods of regular giving, when "Judah rejoiced over the priests and Levites who served" in the days of Zerubbabel and Nehemiah (Neh 12:44-47). But in the interval, when Nehemiah was back in the service of the Persian king, tithing was sporadic at best (Neh 13:10). It was during this time of lapse that Malachi preached so dynamically.

2. The Curse for Robbing God (3:9)

For the third time, the matter of a curse is discussed in Malachi. The first instance concerned a swindler who cheated on a vow (1:14), while the second related to the curse which fell upon the priests (2:2). Now "the whole nation" finds itself under a curse, or more accurately "the curse" of 2:2-3 and Deuteronomy 28:20. It brought blight and famine to the land, as shown in verses 10-11.

Again the Lord states, "You are robbing Me," though the word order is reversed from verse 8. Me you are robbing, your Creator and Father (2:10), the One who redeemed you out of Egypt and entered into an everlasting covenant with you! Robbery is a strange way of expressing gratitude to such a faithful God.

3. The Challenge for Faithful Giving (3:10-12)

a. The Promise of Abundant Divine Blessing (3:10). Faced with the horrible results of their sin, the people are strongly encouraged to change their ways and to turn over their possessions, and thus their hearts, to the Lord. The challenge is to put God first by bringing "the whole tithe into the storehouse, so that there may be food in My house." In Haggai they were exhorted to build God's house; in Malachi, the challenge is to fill His house with food to enable the priests and Levites to perform their ministry properly. God demanded a wholehearted response; *all* of the tithe was needed. Nehemiah may have quoted this verse from Malachi, because he succeeded in getting "all Judah" to bring tithes "into the storehouses" (13:12). The storehouse was the "temple treasury," large rooms into which the tithes were gathered (1 Ki 7:51). Various priests and officials were appointed to distribute the goods for the Levitical service (Neh 12:44; 13:13).

Tithing was viewed as putting God to the test, asking Him to prove His faithfulness once more (Ps 95:9). *Test* is a word used of refining gold (Zec 13:9), an important metaphor in Malachi, since the Messenger of the covenant would "refine them like gold and silver" (3:3). Whenever God's people tested Him by faithful tithing, they discovered that He did bless them abundantly (2 Ch 31:10-11). If we seek first the kingdom of God, and His righteousness "all these things shall be added" to us too (Mt 6:33).

The Lord uses superlative terms in depicting the blessing that He would send to them. Alluding to the Noahic flood, the Lord speaks of opening the windows of heaven and pouring out an overwhelming blessing (Gen 7:11; 8:2). A literal drought was involved in the curse upon the land (see also Hag 1:10-11), as the skies became bronze (Deu 28:23).

Rain was indeed part of the blessing of God, who would open "His good storehouse, the heavens" (Deu 28:12). The word *storehouse,* or *store, treasure* in the last reference is the same Hebrew word found in Malachi 3:10. If men bring tithes into God's storehouse on earth, God will open His storehouse, His treasure in heaven and literally replenish the earth "until there is no more need," or, more precisely, "sufficiency." It refers either to an outpouring that will last until God's resources are exhausted—which is impossible (Ps 72:7)—or until man no longer has any capacity to receive the blessing. The cycle is a complete one. Man fills God's storehouse on earth, receives from God's heavenly storehouse, and lays up "treasures in heaven" (Mt 6:20).

The "windows of heaven" are also mentioned in 2 Kings 7:2 and 19, when Elisha announced a dramatic drop in food prices in the middle of a famine. An official of the king expressed his disbelief by retorting that God would have to make "windows in heaven" to produce such a miracle. During the wilderness wanderings, God in fact "opened" the "doors of heaven" and "rained down manna" to sustain His people (Ps 78:23-24).

Although the New Testament does not specify tithing for believers, the same principles of giving are in effect. To those who give generously, God promises "all sufficiency" and "abundance," terms which may be alluding to Malachi 3:10 (see 2 Co 9:8). "God loves a cheerful giver" (2 Co 9:7), and joy characterized the Jews who, at the dedication of the wall of Jerusalem, "rejoiced over the priests" and brought tithes and contributions (Neh 12:27, 44). Since Abraham gave a tithe to Melchizedek (Gen 14:20) before the Mosaic Law, regular, proportionate giving in the Church age is also a sound principle. God does not change (Mal 3:6). He continues to honor those who are faithful in their giving, and those who "rob God" forfeit tremendous blessing.

b. The Promise of an Abundant Harvest (3:11). Verse 11 further explains how God will reverse the curse of famine if faithful giving is put into practice. Along with sending abundant rains, the Lord will "rebuke the devourer" that has been ruining the crops. This is the opposite of the "rebuke of the seed" mentioned in 2:3 (see extensive comments there and at Hag 1:11). The "devourer" may be the worm that eats up the grapes (Deu 28:39) or the locust that consumes everything in its path (Joel 1:4). In Judges 6:4 the Midianites swarmed over Palestine like locusts, ruining all the crops.

During the famine, the vine was literally "miscarrying," as the unripe grapes fell to the ground. The only other passage that refers to the land "miscarrying" is 2 Kings 2:19 and 21, which describes a city with an impure water supply, causing animals and plants to "miscarry." A drought apparently resulted in the same "dropping" of the grapes. The fruit must "set" or "be formed" properly, or else it will drop off the branches (see Song 2:13). With the end of the dry spell and the absence of destroying insects, the people were assured of excellent crops and a steady income.

c. The Promise of National Prosperity (3:12). The guarantee of God's blessing would enhance the economy and the prestige of the entire nation. Instead of being desolate, the land would again be fertile and a desirable place to live. Israel could again be called "Hephzibah," which means "My delight is in her" (Is 62:4), because God would again find delight in her "as the bridegroom rejoices over the bride" (Is 62:5). In Malachi 1:10 God was not at all pleased with the nation, but if they returned to Him, He would gladly return to them (3:7).

Renewed prosperity would bring Israel a new respect among the nations of the world. Israel would lend money to the nations and would not need to borrow; she would be "the head" and not "the tail" (Deu 28:12-13). As a cursed people, the situation was exactly the reverse (Deu 28:44-45). Back in God's favor, however, Israel would be served by nations (Is 60:12), and her citizens would gain worldwide recognition (Is 61:9). Her relationship with a God of power and of grace would attract many to her land (Zec 8:23).

In the words of Malachi, "All the nations will call you blessed." Just as Leah was called happy at the birth of a son (Gen 30:13), so the people of the world would evaluate Israel's condition as a happy one indeed. Psalm 72:17 expresses the wish that all nations might call the king of Israel blessed (happy), for this is a sign of a powerful and prosperous rule. The same verse refers to the blessing that comes to the nations through Israel, a blessing ultimately brought by the Messiah (Gen 12:3; Hag 2:7).

C. Motivation to Serve the Lord (3:13—4:3)

The promises of verses 10-12 must have sounded attractive to the struggling populace, for they spoke of an enviable prosperity. Yet there were two responses to the Lord's challenge. One group denied the truth of what God said (vv. 13-15), while the other segment of the nation submitted to the Lord in reverential awe (vv. 16-18).

1. *The Charge that Serving God Is Useless* (3:13-15)

a. The Unbelief of the Accusers (3:13). The transition from verse 12 to verse 13 is a difficult one, partially because of the idiom which opens verse 13. Literally, it says, "Your words have been strong against Me," but "strong" in what sense? The expression normally means "to overpower" (2 Ch 8:3; 27:5) or "to win out over" (2 Sa 24:4). David's opinion "prevailed against" Joab or "won out over" Joab in the argument about the need for a census. Perhaps this is the precise sense of 3:13. The skeptical Israelites had introduced their side of the argument in 2:17, where "your words" also occurs. There, they contended that the wicked are more prosperous than the righteous and enjoy God's favor. The Lord had countered this argument with 3:1-12, and especially verses 10-12. But in assessing God's claim, the doubters feel that their case is stronger: their words have "won out over" the Lord's.

Unaware that God has correctly analyzed their thinking, the people instinctively reply, "What have we said about You?" God has, as it were, overheard their conversation and is about to expose their true feelings concerning the claims of verses 10-12 (cf. Eze 33:30).

b. The Nature of the Accusation (3:14-15). Verses 14-15 reveal the motivation of the unbelievers more fully than 2:17, though the arguments are remarkably similar. They charge that serving and worshiping God is useless and unprofitable. Their perspective is essentially selfish: What is our "cut" for serving the Lord? The word *profit* normally has a strong hint of evil (Gen 37:26), showing that they were insincere in their worship of the Lord. Their desire was for personal glory rather than the glorification of God.

Boldly they assert that God has ignored them even though they "have kept His charge." This involves obedience to the commandments, statutes, and laws of God in the noble tradition of Abraham (Gen 26:5). "To keep His charge" means to love God (Deu 11:1) and to avoid all abominations (Lev 18:30). Frequently the idiom is applied to the ministry of priests in the sanctuary (Lev 22:9; 2 Ch 13:11). It was evident from chapters 1 and 2 that the priests were not keeping His charge, and 2:10-16 implicates all the people in flagrant violation of the Law. Sometimes the godly lament that they have been faithful "in vain" (Ps 73:13), when the wicked temporarily prosper. But to have hypocrites offer the same complaint is entirely without justification.

A second empty claim was that they "have walked in mourning" before the Lord to no avail. They donned sackcloth and moved about with blackened faces and garments, sorrowing over the plight of the nation. Like Job they could find no comfort (Job 30:28), for the mourning and fasting (Ps 35:13-14) brought no relief. Apparently they emphasized the external form at the expense of the inner reality. Isaiah also wrote of men who complained that God did not notice when they fasted, attired in appropriate garb. The Lord sharply replied: in a genuine fast the oppressed go free, sins are forsaken, and the poor are cared for (Is 58:2-7; cf. Mal 3:5). Both in Isaiah and in Malachi, the men outwardly humbled themselves before the Lord, but they were only attempting to manipulate Him without true repentance.

Having presented their flimsy evidence, the skeptics reach some startling conclusions which are diametrically opposed to the statements of God in verses 10-12. First, they conclude that the

arrogant are the truly happy ones, not those whose tithing dem-
onstrates a heart of love for God and who are subsequently
prospered before all nations (v. 12). The arrogant are the proud,
the insolent (Pr 21:24), and the presumptuous (Deu 1:41, 43).
They seethe with self-conceit and lash out to oppress (Ps 119:
122) or to murder (Ex 21:14). In Psalm 119:21 the arrogant
are rebuked by God (cf. Mal 3:11) and called "cursed." Those
whom God has cursed, the unbelievers in verse 15 dare to call
"blessed"! In 4:1 the Lord will reply to this blasphemous charge.

Linked with the arrogant, both in verse 15 and in 4:1, are the
"doers of wickedness," a term almost synonymous with "the arrogant." These evildoers are "built up," well-established, and
prosperous. God had plainly said in verse 7, "Return to Me"
and find prosperity, a teaching echoed in Job 22:23: "If you
return to the Almighty, you will be restored" (lit. "built up").
In Jeremiah 12:16, exiled nations are encouraged to learn the
ways of God's people and to swear allegiance to the true God in
order to "be built up." According to the skeptics, however, in
real life wicked men are built up, not the righteous.

As further proof for their claim, the people assert that the
wicked "test God" and get away with it. In verse 10 God had
challenged the nation to put Him to the test through their obedience, but in verse 15 evil men test Him through their rebellion.

During the wilderness wanderings, the Israelites frequently
complained about conditions. They "put God to the test" by asking for food, and the Lord rained down manna (Ex 16:3; Ps
78:18, 24). A short time later, they tested the Lord again, asking
for water (Ex 17:2). Moses struck the rock at Massah, and the
waters poured forth (Ex 17:6-7). Their rebellious testing did
not go unpunished, however, because many died after lusting for
quail (Num 11:33), and the whole generation eventually perished
in the wilderness. Ostensibly they had tested God and escaped,
but in reality such was not the case. The conclusions of verse 15,
like the similar ones in 2:17, are constructed upon a very short-
sighted, superficial view of life.

2. *The Results of Truly Worshiping God* (3:16-18)

a. God Remembers His Own (3:16). An entirely different response to God's challenge of verses 10-12 is found in verses 16-18. The first group had utterly denied the validity of God's promises with words of blasphemy. Now a second group is speaking, not against God (v. 13), but to one another, and their words reflect reverent obedience to the Lord. God "overhears" their conversation also (cf. v. 13) and learns that their worship is genuine and from the heart. As they talked together, they may have been encouraging one another to faithfulness, particularly in light of the godless attitudes of the majority, expressed in verses 13-15.

Twice in the verse, the faithful are called "those who fear the LORD." Throughout the book, God has been looking for those who respect and revere Him (1:6, 11, 14; 2:5; 3:5), and up to this point, none had been found in Israel. Yet there was a remnant true to God, preserved by His grace (3:6).

A corollary to fearing the Lord is to "esteem His name." The priests in particular had been guilty of despising and dishonoring that great name (1:6, 12, 14; 2:2). Finally, here in verse 16, people who truly value His name come on the scene. The interchange between "esteem" and "despise" calls to mind Isaiah 53:3b: "He was despised, and we did not esteem Him." When the Messenger of the covenant entered the world, He experienced to the ultimate degree what it means to be despised and held in low esteem. "He came to His own, and those who were His own did not receive Him" (Jn 1:11).

God was keenly aware of the thoughts and words of the wicked, and He "gave attention and heard" the expressions of reverence spoken by the righteous. Men had scornfully asked, "Where is the God of justice?" (2:17). Verse 16 answers that He is alert and responsive to all the affairs of men. In fact, "A book of remembrance was written before Him" on behalf of the righteous. God kept track of the deeds of men in order to reward them accordingly. As early as Exodus 17:14, God told Moses to record the bitter opposition of the Amalekites "in a book as a memorial." The kings of Israel had books of chronicles written to summarize the accomplishments and events of their reigns (1 Ki 11:41; 14:29).

Persian monarchs also maintained books of records. One such book worked to the advantage of Mordecai, who uncovered a plot against King Ahasuerus, and this was duly recorded in the royal annals (Est 2:23). Some time later, the king was reading this "book of remembrance" during a sleepless night and realized that Mordecai had not yet been rewarded for his heroism (Est 6:1-3). The subsequent reward dramatically affected the status of Mordecai.

God does not have to be prodded by insomnia in order to stir His memory. The divine books are infallibly kept, and some day those books will be opened and the rewards and punishment meted out (Dan 7:10; Rev 20:12). No one who gives a cup of cold water in the name of Christ will lose his reward (Mk 9:41), and those whose names are written in the book of life will enter eternal bliss (Ps 69:28; Is 4:3; Rev 20:12-15).

b. God Spares His Own (3:17-18). Just as the "book of re-membrance" connotes a time of judgment, so does the reference to "day" in verse 17. In 3:2, the subject of "the day of His coming" had been introduced, but the final verses of the book mention "the day" four times (3:17; 4:1, 3, 5). Literally, it is called "the day that I do" or "make" in verse 17 and in 4:3. This common verb is open to many idiomatic usages, and it can be transitive or intransitive. The New American Standard Bible has chosen the rendering "the day that I prepare My own possession." This transitive usage is weakened by the fact that the same con-struction in 4:3 does not have a direct object and because "My" must be supplied to form a smooth translation. An equally valid rendering is, "And they will be my own possession on the day that I take action." (Dan 11:30).[9] Jeremiah 9:7 combines the

9. Compare the translation in the New American Bible and the discussion in Laetsch, pp. 527, 541.

concepts of refining and testing with "doing" in a judgmental
sense, and Malachi has employed the same metaphors in 3:2-3.
God is about to go into action "to punish the inhabitants of the
earth" (Is 26:21).

Those who fear the Lord will be His "own possession." Here
the prophet uses a technical expression that means an "exclusive
possession," or, "valuable property," a "treasure," such as of
silver and gold (1 Ch 29:3; Ec 2:8). The term refers primarily
to the nation of Israel, which God has chosen to be a holy nation
as His private treasure. When God made a covenant with Israel
on Mt. Sinai, they became His own possession (Ex 19:5; Deu
7:6; 14:2; 26:18; Ps 135:4; also see Titus 2:14; 1 Pe 2:9), with
a claim to His protection and blessing.

Only the faithful within the nation are the "true Israel," and
they are the ones who will be spared "as a man spares his own
son." In the words of Psalm 103:13, "Just as a father has compassion on his children, So the LORD has compassion on those
who fear Him." God's people are carefully shielded while the
Lord marches forth in judgment against His enemies (Is 26:20;
Joel 2:18).

The "son who serves him" is the one upon whom the father
takes pity. Children had specific responsibilities to perform for
their parents, and these were viewed as very important. Ugaritic
literature, dating from about the time of Moses, notes that a son
was supposed to defend his father's house from attackers, to
plaster his roof when it leaked, to wash his clothes, and to take
him by the hand when he was drunk.[10] A disrespectful and disobedient son was a disgrace to the family. God's children were
also expected to honor Him (1:6) and to abide by the rules
stated in the covenant. The word translated "serve" is often
rendered "worship" in contexts where the spiritual dimensions
are uppermost (Ex 3:12). By serving God we worship Him, and
worship cannot be divorced from service.

10. The Tale of Aqhat, lines 26-35, translated in James Pritchard, *Ancient Near
    Eastern Texts* (Princeton, N.J.: Princeton U. Press, 1955), p. 150. Com-
    pare also Is 51:18.

On the day of judgment, the difference between the righteous and the wicked, those who serve (worship) God and those who do not, will again be obvious. Their destiny is not the same, and the assertion that God delights in evil men (2:17) will be proved false. The prophet uses "again" because this distinction between the righteous and the wicked had been made before. When God demolished Sodom and Gomorrah, righteous Lot was enabled to escape. His uncle Abraham had interceded for him on the basis that the Judge of all the earth would not "slay the righteous with the wicked" (Gen 18:25). A millennium later, King Asa called on God to be the difference in a battle with the powerful Ethiopians, and the army of Judah was able to rout the enemy (2 Ch 14:11-12).

3. The Coming Day of the Lord (4:1-3)

Additional detail about the coming day, the "day of the Lord," and the distinction between the righteous and the wicked is provided in verses 1-3.[11]

a. The Judgment upon the Wicked (4:1). As in 3:1, "behold" is used to draw attention to the coming of the Lord and the day He takes action. He was to come "like a refiner's fire" in 3:2, while here the day will be "burning like a furnace." In both passages, "the great and terrible day of the LORD" is in view (4:5; see comments on 3:2).

This description is also found in Joel 2:11 and 31, though the translators have rightly selected "awesome" in place of "terrible." "Great" and "awesome" are applied to the name of the Lord in Malachi 1:11 and 14. The Day of the Lord is consistently connected with fire (Joel 2:3, 30), or the burning anger (Is 13:9) and jealousy of the Lord (Zep 1:18). Judgment and fire are thus closely related to the coming of the Lord (Is 66:15-16) and, in particular, to the second coming of Christ "in flaming fire"

---

11. In the Hebrew Bible, chapter 3 has 24 verses; so that 4:1-6 in most English translations equals 3:19-24 according to the Hebrew numbering.

(2 Th 1:7). At the close of the Millennium, fire will consume Gog and Magog also (Rev 20:9).

The "furnace" here in 4:1 is sometimes used of an oven for baking. "Burning" has the sense of a "heated oven" in Hosea 7:4. Psalm 21:9 associates the anger of God with a "fiery oven" to consume His enemies. An oven can also symbolize the presence of God (Gen 15:17). Whether "oven" or "furnace" be preferred, the point of the comparison is the intensity of the heat. It is white hot and destroys quickly and completely (Dan 3:22).

The fiery judgment is directed against the arrogant and the wicked, whom the skeptics called happy and prosperous in 3:15. Their heralded "escape" from God's judgment proves to be short-lived, as they and their "prosperity" are burned up like chaff or stubble. Chaff burns with great rapidity and frequently appears in contexts that relate to judgment (Ex 15:7; Is 5:24; Ob 18). John the Baptist probably had this passage in mind when he announced that Jesus would "burn up the chaff with unquenchable fire" (Mt 3:10, 12; see notes on 3:2).

To underscore the effectiveness of this blaze, the Lord declares that it will leave "neither root nor branch." Using the common metaphor of a tree or vine, God illustrates how completely the wicked will be wiped out. Not to have root or branch means that the posterity and memory of the ungodly will be cut off (Job 18:16-19) by the "flame" against "all the trees of the field" (Joel 1:19). There is no further chance of growth or bearing fruit (Eze 17:8-9). In Obadiah 18, Edom is compared to stubble set on fire by the house of Jacob, with the result that "there will be no survivor" for the people of Esau. How bleak is the future of the enemies of God!

b. The Triumph of the Righteous (4:2-3). For those who fear the Lord and His great name (cf. 3:16), the future is extremely bright. It will not be the brightness of a consuming fire, however, as in verse 1, but the shining of the sun of righteousness with healing in its wings. The interpretation of this metaphor is difficult: does the "sun" refer to God, and perhaps the "Son," or is it only a personification of the "sun" without implying Deity?

Several factors indicate that God in Christ is indeed the point of the illustration. Many times God is compared to the sun or to light in the Old Testament. In Isaiah 60:2, the Lord is said to "rise upon you" in His glory, and toward the end of the chapter, the Lord is described as "an everlasting light" to replace the sun (Is 60:19-20). Psalm 84:11 says that God is "a sun and shield," providing for the growth and blessing of His children.

The relationship between God and the sun is an extremely important one, because the sun, so vital to the whole life cycle, was worshiped throughout the Near East, for instance, as "Re" in Egypt and "Shamash" in Babylon. Genesis 1 declares that God created the sun and is thus greater than the light in the heavens. To prevent sun worship, the Temple was oriented in an East-West direction, so that men would face away from the sun as they worshiped God (cf. Eze 8:16). This East-West orientation also symbolized the rule of God over the entire world. Just as the sun ran its course across the sky from East to West, so the Lord was in complete control "from the rising of the sun, even to its setting" (Mal 1:11; cf. Ps 19:4-6). No spot on earth could escape His all-seeing gaze.

Christ in His coming is called a "great light" to shine upon those in darkness (Is 9:2; 42:6; 49:6). In Luke 1, Zacharias ties together Malachi 4:2 and Isaiah 9:2 in an apparent Messianic reference (Lk 1:76, 78, 79). The father of John the Baptist mentions the coming of the "Sunrise from on high" (Lk 1:78), using the noun form of the word *arise,* found in the Greek Old Testament (*anatelei* in the Septuagint) here in Malachi. Another Messianic passage refers to the "star" out of Jacob (Num 24:17), and Peter combines the concepts of the day dawning and the morning star arising (2 Pe 1:19).

The "healing in its wings" has reference to the rays of the sun as they rapidly spread light and warmth over the countryside.[12] Psalm 139:9 speaks of "the wings of the dawn" in an analogous figure. Since *wings,* however, when applied to God, usually describes the protection and refuge found "in the shadow" of His wings (Ps 57:1), it is possible that a mixed metaphor is in view here as in the preceding verse. Psalm 84:11 does say that God is "a sun and shield," making the same difficult connection (cf. Ps 91:4).

Within the metaphor, "healing" and "righteousness" are related concepts. The godly have apparently been oppressed and afflicted while the arrogant have prospered. Like Job, the righteous may have wondered when the God of healing would intervene. Already the skeptics had asked, "Where is the God of justice?" In 4:2 we learn that the God of righteousness and justice will appear on behalf of the godly. "Righteousness" obviously connotes the fairness and strictness of God's work as judge, but it also involves the consequences of His righteous character and judgment for His people, namely, salvation. "Righteousness" is often parallel to "salvation" in Scripture (Is 51:5, 6, 8) and hence takes on the meaning of deliverance.

Such deliverance can ultimately be based only on the substitutionary death of Christ, who clothes us in His righteousness as we believe in Him (Is 53:11). Through the sacrifice of Christ, we can be healed (Is 53:5). The spiritual aspects of salvation and healing are linked with the physical in the first coming of Christ. Our Lord Himself quoted from Isaiah 61:1-2, for He was the One who brought good news to the afflicted and proclaimed liberty to captives (Lk 4:18-19), healing diseased bodies and souls in His ministry.

This "liberty to captives" is pictured by the leaping of calves from the stall in verse 2. Some animals were kept in confine-

12. The winged sun disk was common on Near Eastern monuments. Note plate 351, the Black Obelisk of Shalmaneser, and plate 477 from Byblos in Pritchard, *The Ancient Near East in Pictures* (Princeton, N.J.: Princeton U., 1954). Also see Joyce Baldwin, *Haggai, Zechariah, Malachi,* p. 250.

ment so that they might be fattened and slaughtered for a feast (Amos 6:4). If released, they would skip about joyfully, frolicking in their new freedom. Similar is the reaction of people no longer shackled by sickness (Ac 3:8) or oppression. The Lord "heals the brokenhearted and binds up their wounds" (Ps 147:3).

Ultimately the healing work of Christ looks ahead to the second coming of Christ, when the godly remnant of Israel will be restored to "health and healing" (Jer 33:6). "Healing" means "deliverance from destruction" in Psalm 107:20, and this is the primary meaning in Malachi. This passage, like 3:1-3, is a blend of the first and second coming of Christ, with emphasis upon the latter event.

The infusion of health and strength from the Sun of righteousness will so empower the righteous that they will trample the wicked, reduced to powder by the consuming flame of God (4:1). Those who were once so proud, so arrogant (3:13-15), will become nothing more than a pile of ashes. This was also the fate of the high and mighty king of Tyre, who was consumed and disgraced before the eyes of the nations (Eze 28:18). Cities that seem unassailable are brought down to the dust to be trampled underfoot.

In Isaiah 63:1-6, Christ treads the winepress in His day of vengeance, staining His clothes with the blood of the nations. Since the word *tread* in Malachi is cognate to a word for "wine," the imagery may be similar (cf. Ps 58:10). The day on which the righteous tread down the wicked is the day the Lord finally takes action. (See comments on 3:17 for "take action.")

D. Conclusion (4:4-6)

1. *The Challenge to Keep the Law of Moses* (4:4)

This last paragraph forms the conclusion to the entire book, though particularly to the section on the coming of God's Messenger. "Remember the law of Moses!" If the people wanted to avoid being condemned by a righteous and powerful God, they should join the ranks of those who reverence the Lord.

The Law of Moses, which dealt with religion, politics, society, and the family, had been badly neglected by the priests and the people. They had turned aside from the instruction of the statutes and ordinances (2:8; 3:7), and the curses of God plagued the nation. Moses warned them to observe the entire Law so that they could take possession of Canaan and prosper in the land (Deu 1:1, 5, 8, 14). Yet the nation neglected the Law; they did not remember, but God did, and kept a "book of remembrance" (3:16) to record their deeds.

Here at the close of the Old Testament period, Malachi gives the nation one more chance to remember, to obey the Law before it is too late. This final plea is reinforced by an appeal to the divine authority of the Law. Moses was *God's* servant, and *God* had given the statutes and ordinances to Israel through Moses. The revelation had occurred on Horeb, the mountain of God (Ex 3:1). Better known as Mt. Sinai, because of its location in the desert of Sinai (Ex 19:1), this holy mountain was shaken by thunder and lightning as the God of majesty came down to converse with Moses (Ex 19:16). Through Malachi, the same awesome God was calling all Israel to serve Him.

2. *The Coming and Work of Elijah* (4:5-6)

Vital to the message of the book is the sending of "My messenger" and "the Lord," "the Messenger of the covenant" (3:1). The Lord, in verse 5, reemphasizes the importance of that "sending" and introduces the name of Elijah the prophet, who also met with God on Mt. Horeb (1 Ki 19:8). Clearly there is a relationship between 3:1 and 4:5 because of the repetition of "behold," the participial "I am sending," and the similarity of the mission. Both "to clear the way" and "to restore" are based on verbs that imply "turning." In addition, "My messenger" doubles as a proper name "Malachi" (see 3:1), and the sending of "My messenger" and of "Elijah" is followed by a reference to the awesome Day of the Lord (3:2; 4:5).

Faced with this evidence, many have concluded that "Elijah"

is simply another name for John the Baptist. *Levi* is used in 2:
4-8 to refer to the later Levitical priests, so *Elijah* could represent men who resembled that great prophet. Support for this
view is found in Luke 1:17, where Gabriel informs Zacharias
that John the Baptist will minister "in the spirit and power of
Elijah," "To turn the hearts of the fathers back to the children,"
citing Malachi 4:6. Christ Himself agreed with this identification when He said, "Elijah already came, and they did not recognize him" (Mt 11:13-14; 17:12). The disciples correctly understood that He was referring to John the Baptist (Mt 17:13).
When John denied that he was Elijah (Jn 1:21), he simply
meant that he was not literally the same person back on earth
once again. Even his dress and style of ministry were similar to
Elijah's (2 Ki 1:8; Mt 3:4).

The identification of John the Baptist with Elijah is thus very
convincing, but the possibility remains that it does not exhaust
the full meaning of this prophecy. After all, John did not come
immediately before "the great and terrible day of the LORD" mentioned in Malachi (see comments on 4:1 for this term). Previous
passages have also blended references to the first and second
coming of Christ (3:1-4; 4:1-3).

Prior to the second coming, Revelation speaks of two witnesses
(11:3) who will minister with great authority for 1260 days.
Some interpreters have identified these two men with Moses and
Elijah and view their ministry as a fulfillment of Malachi 4:4-6,
which does mention Moses and Elijah in successive verses. The
men are called "prophets" in Revelation 11:10, and they are
capable of preventing rain, turning water into blood, and smiting
the earth with plagues (Rev 11:6).

During their careers, Elijah and Moses were enabled to perform these very miracles. Moses and Elijah also appeared together on the mount of transfiguration (Mt 17:3; Mk 9:4), perhaps an indication of their future ministry.[13] Jewish tradition cer-

13. For a fuller discussion of the witnesses in Revelation, see J. B. Smith,
    A Revelation of Jesus Christ (Scottdale, Pa.: Herald, 1961), pp. 169-70.

tainly favored a literal return of Elijah (Jn 1:21), and Christ said not only that Elijah has come but, "Elijah is coming and will restore all things" (Mt 17:11). This may be looking beyond John the Baptist. The terminology of Matthew 11:14 also hints that John was "Elijah" in a limited way: "And if you care to accept it, he himself is Elijah." The interpretation of both passages is difficult, however.

The task of John the Baptist, and perhaps of Elijah himself in the future, was to effect a reconciliation between fathers and sons. Luke 1:17 explains the turning of the hearts of the children to their fathers as "the disobedient [turning] to the attitude of the righteous." Most likely, "the fathers" refers to the godly ancestors of Israel, men like the patriarchs and David, whose lives were committed to God. "The children" were their disobedient descendants who, like Malachi's generation, had strayed far from the faith. When John the Baptist preached the baptism of repentance to prepare a people for the Lord (Lk 1:17), he was calling his contemporaries to the attitude of confession and trust that characterized the greats of old.

Earlier in Malachi 3:7, God had implored the people, "Return to Me, and I will return to you." The same basic verb, meaning "to cause to turn" or "restore" appears in 4:6. If the children repent of their sin, their relationship with God and with their fathers will be restored. Their heart attitude will be in tune with the faith of Abraham (cf. Mt 3:9).

Resistance to the plea of God's messenger would bring a terrible curse upon the land. Malachi has mentioned curses in three previous passages (1:14; 2:2; 3:9), but this is the first time that so strong a term has been employed. Often translated "ban," this curse involves extermination, the total destruction of persons and goods.

The Canaanite peoples were placed "under the ban," to wipe out any influence of their corrupt culture upon the Israelites (Deu 20:17-18). This meant that all the people were to be killed and all the goods burned. Only the silver and gold and the

articles of bronze and iron could be preserved, and these were
dedicated to the Lord, the exclusive property of the treasury of
the Lord (Jos 6:17-19). This exclusiveness is illustrated by the
English word *harem,* which is derived from the Hebrew *herem.*
A harem was set apart, off-limits, and everyone except the owner
was banned from the premises.

Israelite cities were subject to the ban if they were apostate
(Deu 13:16-17), and in Isaiah 43:28, God speaks of consigning
Jacob to the ban. In all probability this has reference to the destruction of Jerusalem and the Temple (Ps 79:1-4), when God
temporarily abandoned His people. The Roman conquest of
Jerusalem in AD 70 may have been the curse that followed the
Jews' rejection of Christ, though at His second coming, Christ
will smite the nations and tread the winepress of His wrath (Rev
19:15; cf. Mal 4:3).

It constitutes a horrible alternative to repentance and faith,
but the powerful language was intended to instill godly fear in
the hearts of men.

The Masoretes, Jewish scholars who preserved the Hebrew
Bible during the Middle Ages, repeated verse 5 after verse 6,
lest the book of the twelve minor prophets end on the harsh note
of a curse. This attempt to soften the message does not alter the
grim reality.

The concluding verses of Malachi offer a great opportunity to
return to God and the Law of Moses. Throughout the book, the
Lord had been searching for people who would genuinely respect
Him. Yet, influenced by contemptuous leaders, the whole worship of the Temple was allowed to deteriorate badly. Israelites
were contracting "marriages" with foreign gods while breaking
up their own families. They thought that God did not care
whether they were good or bad. How they lived made little difference, so they kept on sinning and robbing God of devotion and
tithes and offerings. Since God did not seem to take action
against the wicked, they gave little thought to the possibility that
He might "suddenly come to His temple" to settle accounts.

Sad to say, the attitudes of ancient Israel are all too common in the modern world. In this day of political scandals, one sees the curse of leaders who have betrayed the public trust. Dishonesty, bribery, and irreverence abound, and God seems much more of a slogan than a reality. Even church members are so married to the world and its values that the coming of Christ is a hazy possibility at best. Dedicated leaders within the Church are as rare as in Malachi's day. Few worry about God's "book of remembrance." God's patience must be exhausted as He sees the collapse of marriages and lack of commitment to His work.

Surrounded by convicting evidence, the world can nevertheless rejoice that God's gracious invitation, extended through Malachi, still holds today. The God who urged Israel to return to Him promises to turn in saving power to any who will fear and believe Him. All who take His Word seriously and obey His commands can experience an outpouring of blessing today and can look forward to Christ's coming with joyful anticipation. The unbelieving world will feel the awesome judgment of the Day of the Lord, but His servants will rule with Him victoriously. When the kingdoms of this world are overthrown (Hag 2:22), those whose bodies are the temple of the Holy Spirit will enjoy His presence forever.

Bibliography

Baldwin, Joyce G. *Haggai, Zechariah, Malachi.* Downers Grove, Ill.: Inter-Varsity, 1972.

Feinberg, Charles L. "Haggai." In *Wycliffe Bible Commentary.* Chicago: Moody, 1962.

Freeman, Hobart E. *An Introduction to the Old Testament Prophets.* Chicago. Moody, 1968.

Gaebelein, Frank E. *Four Minor Prophets.* Chicago: Moody, 1970.

Goddard, Burton L. "Malachi." In *Wycliffe Bible Commentary.* Chicago: Moody, 1962.

Greathouse, William M. "Malachi." In *Beacon Bible Commentary.* Vol. 5. Kansas City, Mo.: Beacon Hill, 1966.

Harrison, R. K. *Introduction to the Old Testament.* Grand Rapids: Eerdmans, 1969.

Keil, Carl Friedrich. *The Twelve Minor Prophets.* Vol. 2. Reprint. Grand Rapids: Eerdmans, 1949.

Laetsch, Theodore. *The Minor Prophets.* St. Louis: Concordia, 1956.

Lewis, Jack P. *The Minor Prophets.* Grand Rapids: Baker, 1966.

May, Herbert G. " 'This People' and 'This Nation' in Haggai." *Vetus Testamentum* 18 (1968):190-97.

McCurdy, James. "The Book of Haggai." In *A Commentary on the Holy Scriptures.* Ed. by John Lange and Philip Schaff. New York: Scribner, Armstrong, 1875.

Packard, Joseph. "The Book of Malachi." In *A Commentary on the Holy Scripture.* Ed. by John Lange and Philip Schaff. New York: Scribner, Armstrong, 1875.

Pusey, E. B. *The Minor Prophets.* Vol. 2. New York: Funk & Wagnalls, 1885.

Schultz, Samuel J. *The Prophets Speak.* New York: Harper & Row, 1968.

Siebeneck, R. T. "The Messianism of Aggeus and Proto-Zacharias." *Catholic Biblical Quarterly* 19 (1957).

Wolff, Richard. *The Book of Haggai.* Grand Rapids: Baker, 1967.